Improving Connections Between Governments and Nonprofit and Voluntary Organizations

Public Policy and the Third Sector

Improving Connections Between Governments and Nonprofit and Voluntary Organizations

Public Policy and the Third Sector

Edited by Kathy L. Brock

Published for the School of Policy Studies, Queen's University
by McGill-Queen's University Press
Montreal & Kingston • London • Ithaca

National Library of Canada Cataloguing in Publication Data

Main entry under title:

Improving connections between governments and nonprofit and voluntary organizations : public policy and the third sector

Papers from a conference held Oct. 20-21, 2000, Queen's University, Kingston, Ont.
Includes bibliographical references.
ISBN 0-88911-907-4 (bound).—ISBN 0-88911-899-X (pbk.)

1. Nonprofit organizations—Government policy—Canada. 2. Voluntarism—Government policy—Canada. 3. Canada—Social policy. I. Brock, Kathy Lenore, 1958-   II. Queen's University (Kingston, Ont.). School of Policy Studies

HD2769.2.C3146 2002   361.7'63'0971   C2001-904058-X

CONTENTS

PREFACE

The first annual National Forum on the Third Sector and Public Policy was held at the School of Policy Studies, Queen's University, 20–21 October 2000. Each year the forum explores a different theme of national importance to the sector. This year it was "Improving Connections between Governments and Nonprofit and Voluntary Organisations." The objective of the national forum was to bring together academics and practitioners from the third sector and governments at a national conference to contribute to developing a better understanding of the evolving relationship between governments and the nonprofit and voluntary sector in Canada. The conference facilitated the discussion of ideas across jurisdictions and the exchange of traditional research with experiential knowledge so as to help create a dialogue between the sectors. This type of forum is very important in the wake of the National Research Symposium held in Banff, 8–10 September 2000, where it was concluded that the three sectors needed to exchange ideas and information to assist in the production of research. The forum complements the work of the Voluntary Sector Initiative (VSI) by offering a venue for the exchange of experiences and ideas independent of government and the third sector organizations.

The conference was designed to examine the relationships between the governments and the voluntary sector at the federal, provincial, and territorial levels and to incorporate the perspectives of government officials, third sector representatives and academics. The three keynote speakers were selected to highlight future trends in the sector (Chief Charity Commissioner of England and Wales, John Stoker), to situate the Canadian experience in an international context (Secretary-General of CARE International, Guy Tousignant), and to reflect upon the future of the relationship (Minister of Community Development, Cooperatives and Volunteers BC, Jenny Kwan).

The forum was a success according to the evaluations and informal comments of participants. The exchange of ideas and experiences was lively, poignant, and meaningful. Representatives from the three sectors (governments, voluntary, and academic) gained a deeper appreciation of how the challenges involved in building a stronger relationship affect both government and third sector actors and how these experiences vary across the country. Some important lessons may be drawn from these exchanges. That is why it was important that this information and research be compiled into a book and shared more widely among the three communities in Canada.

Therefore, the objective of publishing and disseminating the conference proceedings is to foster the exchange of information and ideas across jurisdictions and sectors in Canada. At present, there is a lack of knowledge of what different communities and government are doing to promote the third sector, build its capacity, and improve the delivery of services to Canadians. The conference began that dialogue. The book makes that exchange available to a broader community than was able to attend the conference. In particular, smaller organizations, academics, and government officials not able to attend the forum will be able to share in this rich dialogue.

And thus, I have five modest hopes for this book:

- *To build the research capacity of the third sector.* The proceedings provide a rich source of original data that may assist researchers within the sector in building an understanding of developments at the national level as well as within their provinces and to learn about issues and new developments in other jurisdictions.

- *To assist in the instruction and training of academic researchers on the third sector for the future study of third sector and government relations and issues.* At present many academics are working on subjects related to the third sector (e.g., interest groups, state-society relations, nongovernmental organizations, civil society, social capital, trust) but do not define their research as falling within this area. This book makes these linkages more evident and might even encourage scholars to explore third sector issues more directly. The variety of perspectives and issues discussed at the conference might also encourage more interdisciplinary dialogue on the sector.

- *To facilitate classroom learning and the training of current and future researchers and leaders.* The book is a potentially valuable text for executive training programs for government and third sector officials and managers, and for graduate seminars on the study of the third sector. It would also be a useful resource for undergraduate and graduate research papers.

- *To assist in the development of a corpus of literature on the third sector which is underdeveloped at present in Canada.* The speakers and topics of the forum were carefully chosen to supplement gaps in the research on the third sector and its relationship with government. It is genuinely hoped that this book will contribute to the existing body of knowledge, but also be an important building-block in the construction of an informed body of research on the third sector.

- *To help build better relationships between governments and the third sector.* In particular, the two case studies of why relationships work will be instructive for government officials and third sector organizations as they endeavour to create productive relationships over a wider array of areas than in the past.

In sum, my desire is that this publication will assist the (i) third sector by providing a fertile resource on developments nationally and in other jurisdictions across Canada, (ii) government actors by providing access to the views and concerns of third sector representatives, and (iii) academics and the academic community by increasing awareness of issues facing the third sector and the experiences of practitioners. The book will be especially valuable to both government and third sector members of the VSI as they work together to foster a new relationship in Canada.

The forum was the first of three forums to be held as part of the Public Policy and Third Sector Initiative at the School of Policy Studies, Queen's University. This initiative was established with the support of the Kahanoff Foundation to encourage new research and critical reflection on issues facing governments and the third sector in Canada as they strive to redefine and strengthen their relationships with the objective of serving Canadians better. The mandate of the School's Public Policy and Third Sector Initiative is to educate current and prospective government officials about third sector issues and educate current and prospective leaders in the third sector about government and the importance of the changing policy environment to their organizations; to develop a national network of scholars to explore critically the interactions between governments and the third sector; and to encourage research and the exchange of ideas across Canada on the relationship between the third sector and government from a variety of perspectives.

This book reflects the contributions of many people and organizations. The conference was lively and stimulating. For that I am indebted to the conference speakers who gave so generously of their time and ideas and to the participants who made a special effort to attend, to listen, to debate, and to share their ideas in the question and answer sessions, over coffee, and at the social gatherings. The conference could not have taken place without the generous support of the Kahanoff Foundation and I would especially like to thank the Vice-President, Shira Herzog. The School of Policy Studies supplemented the conference and proceedings while the Institute for Research on Public Policy (IRPP) hosted the dinner for all conference participants. Information about the conference was helpfully disseminated by the Voluntary Sector Task Force, Canada West Foundation, the Canadian Centre for Philanthropy, the Coalition of National Voluntary Organisations, and Charity Village. The members of the Public Policy and Third Sector Advisory Board offered sensible direction in constructing the agenda. Lois Jordan and Todd Yates were assiduous in attending to the administrivia necessary for running a conference. The student volunteers, led by Danielle Koster and David Adames, were a large part of its success by offering help as needed and a touch of professionalism that was felt by all. Shirley Fraser transcribed the proceedings and Louis Kwabena Anone and Danielle Koster provided preliminary research and editing assistance on the initial transcripts. Mark Howes, Valerie Jarus and Marilyn Banting of the School of Policy Studies Publications Unit were as scrupulous as ever in the preparation of the manuscript.

However, the book would not have been possible without a generous contribution agreement from Human Resources Development Canada. Marilyn Redmond helped guide the funding and provided support and encouragement as the manuscript became a book. All these efforts, and the contributions of others, are deeply appreciated. But an especially warm thank you must go to my friends who encouraged me when I decided to move mid-career to Queen's University to take up a new challenge and who understood the importance of the conference in that decision. They also taught me that the best way to finish a conference is with friends, laughter, red wine and pizza; so to Leanne Matthes, Miyo Yamashita, Terry Goertzen, and especially Steve Streeter, thanks.

And lastly, this work is dedicated to my father who gave sage advice and then listened eagerly to my stories about the conference but did not live to read the book.

CONTRIBUTORS

PADDY BOWEN is Executive Director of Volunteer Canada. She has had 20 years experience in the sector, beginning on the frontlines with service delivery for youth and rising through a series of positions from service delivery to national leader. She served for a number of years as Executive Director of Home Support Canada and has held her current position for five years. She is currently serving on the committees for the National Volunteers Initiative and the International Year of Volunteers (2001).

KATHY L. BROCK is Associate Professor and Head of Public Policy and the Third Sector at the School of Policy Studies, Queen's University. She was a tenured Associate Professor at Wilfrid Laurier University from 1995 to 1999 and an assistant and then tenured Associate Professor at the University of Manitoba from 1988 to 1995. Dr. Brock has served as an advisor to then-Grand Chief Phil Fontaine of the Assembly of Manitoba Chiefs, to politicians on political and constitutional issues, and is currently an advisor to the Manitoba Minister of Aboriginal and Northern Affairs Eric Robinson and a documentalist and occasional advisor to the Joint Coordinating Committee of the Voluntary Sector Initiative. She has written numerous articles and chapters on interest groups and the constitutional process, federalism, the voluntary sector, and Aboriginal issues, and has recently co-edited a book on *The Nonprofit Sector in a New Century*.

DAVID CAMERON is Professor of Political Science at the University of Toronto. He began his career at Trent University, where he was Chair of the Department of Political Studies and Dean of Arts and Science. He served as Director of Research for the Pepin-Robarts Task Force on Canadian Unity in 1977 and joined the Government of Canada in 1979 as an Advisor in the Federal-Provincial Relations Office. Dr. Cameron came to the University of Toronto, first as a Vice-President of Institutional Relations and after a period in the Ontario government as Deputy Minister of Intergovernmental Affairs, returned to join the Political Science Department in 1990. He has written numerous articles, chapters, and books on federalism, nationalism, Quebec and citizen engagement. His recent book is co-authored with Graham White, *Cycling into Saigon: The 1995 Conservative Transition in Ontario.*

SUSAN CARTER is Executive Director of the Voluntary Sector Secretariat established by the Voluntary Sector Roundtable. She was Associate Director of the Canadian Council on Social Development from 1995 to 1999. Before joining the Council, she had worked in the federal public service in a number of departments including Human Resources Development, Health, and the Privy Council Office. She has been closely involved in the founding and creation of the Voluntary Sector Roundtable, the Panel on Accountability and Governance in the Voluntary Sector, the Joint Tables on the Voluntary Sector, and the Voluntary Sector Initiative.

ARTHUR DRACHE currently practises law with the firm of Drache Burke-Robertson & Buchmayer. He is best known in Canada as the contributing editor to *The Financial Post,* writing more than 1,100 articles and opinion pieces, and winning the National Business Writing Award. He has served as counsel to the House of Commons Committee on Communications and Culture pertaining to the taxation of arts and artists, to the Senate Committee on Banking Trade and Commerce and as a member of Revenue Canada's advisory group on charities. He is the editor of two reference books on charities and taxation and a monthly newsletter, *Canadian Not-for-Profit News.* He has written, contributed to or co-authored over 12 books, including *Non-Share Capital Corporations* with Jane Burke-Robertson. He is acknowledged as a leading expert in the tax treatment of charities and nonprofit organizations and the taxation of the arts and artists.

SUSAN FLETCHER is Executive Director of the Voluntary Sector Task Force in the Privy Council Office of the federal government. She provides advice and support to a group of nine ministers and to senior officials in the Privy Council Office and in 24 departments on the development of governmentwide policies and strategies affecting the voluntary sector. Previously, she was an Account Executive with the Public Service Commission. She joined the public service in 1970 and has served in a number of positions in Statistics Canada, Finance, and Health.

HAL GEREIN was appointed Deputy Minister of the Ministry of Community Development, Cooperatives and Volunteers in British Columbia in May 2000, having joined the ministry in 1999. He has held a number of positions in various BC ministries, including the BC Ministry of Forests. Previously, he was a Deputy Minister of Education, Culture and Employment and Assistant Deputy Minister of Municipal and Community Affairs in the Northwest Territories. He worked as a professional planner in Northern Alberta and the Northwest Territories and as a consultant in planning to Vocha, Komi Republic in Russia. He has extensive experience working with business, labour, consumers, voluntary groups, and with First Nations. He is currently with Gerein & Associates, Planning, Leadership & Management Consulting.

TERRY GOERTZEN was the Special Advisor to the Minister of Health in Manitoba. On leave from the City of Winnipeg, he provided strategic and communications counsel in the political, public, and nonprofit sectors. He received his Bachelor of Education from the University of Winnipeg and taught in a high school work education program. He was hired to provide research for the Opposition NDP in 1990 and was appointed to the position of Special Assistant and Communications Coordinator for the Opposition Leader Gary Doer. After serving as Press Secretary for the 1995 provincial election campaign, Mr. Goertzen entered the nonprofit sector as the publicist for the Manitoba Theatre Centre and Director of Marketing, Winnipeg Fringe Theatre Festival. In 1998, he was employed by the City of Winnipeg as Manager of Public Affairs, providing strategic communications counsel for the administration. He is currently Director of Public Affairs, Government Relations, Winnipeg Regional Health Authority.

KATHERINE GRAHAM is Professor and Associate Dean in the Faculty of Public Affairs and Management at Carleton University. Dr. Graham has been active for over 20 years as a researcher and consultant on local government. Her work has involved studies of local politics and administration across Canada and abroad, and as a consultant. In 1990, the Ontario Minister of Municipal Affairs appointed her Commissioner of Election Boundaries for the Regional Municipality of Ottawa-Carleton. Her major recommendations were implemented through provincial legislation, taking effect with the 1994 municipal elections.

MICHAEL HALL is Vice-President Research at the Canadian Centre for Philanthropy and Director of the Kahanoff Foundation's Nonprofit Sector Research Initiative. His many publications on nonprofit sector topics include *Charitable*

Fundraising in Canada and *Caring Canadians, Involved Canadians: Highlights from the National Survey of Giving, Volunteering and Participating.* He is an associate editor of *Nonprofit Management and Leadership* and holds a PhD in social psychology from York University.

ALAN J. (AL) HATTON is Executive Director of the Coalition of National Voluntary Organisations (NVO) and has actively participated in the voluntary sector both nationally and internationally for over 30 years. His involvement ranges from working with youth (Verdun Council of Community Agencies) to various senior management positions such as National Director of Job Generation and Director of External Relations within the YMCA. A founding member of the Voluntary Sector Roundtable, he also co-chaired the Building a New Relationship Joint Table of the PCO Process that resulted in the *Working Together Report.* He sits on the board of the Youth Services Bureau of Ottawa-Carleton and is a member of the Brazil Steering Committee of United Way of Canada/Centraide Canada.

RAINER KNOPFF is Professor of Political Science at the University of Calgary. He was educated at McMaster University and the University of Toronto. Dr. Knopff has published widely in the areas of public law, human rights, and Canadian political thought. His books include *Human Rights and Social Technology: The New War on Discrimination* (with T.E. Flanagan), *Charter Politics* (with F.L. Morton), and *The Charter Revolution and the Court Party* (with F.L. Morton). He is currently working on a new book entitled *Courting Controversy.*

JENNY KWAN was appointed Minister of Community Development, Co-operatives and Volunteers in February 2000 for the NDP government of British Columbia. She graduated from the Criminology Department of Simon Fraser University and worked as a community activist in the Downtown Eastside. She was the youngest person elected to Vancouver City Council in 1993 and served for three years. She was one of the first Chinese-Canadian women elected to the Legislative Assembly in British Columbia and has served as Deputy Whip to the Government Caucus, Parliamentary Secretary to the Minister of Health, a member of the Select Standing Committee for Public Accounts and the Special Committee on the Response to the Gove Report. She was appointed Minister of Municipal Affairs in 1998, and then served as Minister of Women's Equality, 1999–2000.She is currently the NDP MLA for Vancouver Mount Pleasant.

PETER LEVESQUE is the Program Officer for the Community-University Research Alliances pilot program at SSHRC. He is a member of the board of the Loka Institute, based in Amherst, Massachusetts and is a PhD candidate in Public Policy at the School for Public Administration at Carleton University. His experience includes four years in community and economic development and over seven years in the insurance, manufacturing, and retail sectors. Areas of enquiry include management of research infrastructure, domestic and international cross-sector collaboration, social capital, collective values, philanthropy and fundraising, and sustainability.

PETER MILLIKEN is the Member of Parliament for Kingston and the Islands. He was appointed Deputy Speaker of the House of Commons and Chairman of the Committees of the Whole House in 1997. As a member of the Liberal government from 1993, Mr. Milliken served as Parliamentary Secretary to the Government House Leader, Chairman of the Standing Committee on Procedure and House Affairs and Co-Chair of the Special Joint Committee on a Code of Conduct. In 1996, he was named Deputy Chairman of Committees of the Whole House. First elected to the House of Commons in 1988, Mr. Milliken held several positions in opposition, including Party Critic for Election Reform and Associate Critic for Seniors, Assistant Party House Leader (House Business), Vice-Chairman of the Special Committee on Electoral Reform and Member of the Standing Committee on House Management. On 29 January 2001, he was elected 34th Speaker of the House of Commons.

PATRICK MONAHAN is Professor of Law at Osgoode Hall Law School of York University. He has written widely on issues related to constitutional law, public policy and institutions of government and is a frequent commentator in the national media. He has often been retained to advise major public sector organizations, including the Government of Canada, various provincial and municipal governments, federal Royal Commissions, government agencies, the Auditor General of Canada and the Law Society of Upper Canada. He is also an Affiliated Scholar with the law firm Davies, Ward & Beck in Toronto and has appeared as counsel before a variety of courts and tribunals, including the Supreme Court of Canada.

MONICA PATTEN is President and CEO of Community Foundations of Canada, the member organization for Canada's 103 community foundations.

She was previously a Vice-President of United Way of Canada/Centraide Canada, and Executive Director of Ottawa's Volunteer Centre. She is a board member of the Centre for Voluntary Sector Research and Development of Ottawa and Carleton Universities, and has served on the Conference Board of Canada's Committee on Benchmarking of corporate social responsibility. She remains active with the Canadian Centre for Philanthropy's Imagine Program. She co-chaired the Joint Table on Strengthening Capacity in the federal-voluntary sector exercise that produced the *Working Together* Report and currently sits on the Joint Coordinating Committee of the Voluntary Sector Initiative. She is active in several international initiatives to promote philanthropy and strengthen civil society.

VIVIAN RANDELL was Assistant Secretary to Cabinet (Social Policy) in the Executive Council of the Government of Newfoundland and Labrador. She has been assigned management responsibility for the implementation of the province's Strategic Social Plan. Employed with the provincial public service for 29 years in a variety of positions, she has served as provincial Child Adoptions' Officer, Acting Assistant Director of Child Welfare, Director of Staff Development, Director of Day-Care and Homemakers' Services, and Director of Policy and Planning, all in the Department of Human Resources. She is a registered social worker holding a BA and BSW from Memorial University and an MA (Social Welfare Policy) from McMaster University. She is currently Deputy Minister, Department of Human Resources and Employment, Government of Newfoundland and Labrador.

PENELOPE ROWE is CEO Community Services Council, Newfoundland and Labrador. She chaired the Workplace Health Safety and Compensation Commission of Newfoundland and Labrador for 11 years. She was instrumental in the development of the Government of Newfoundland and Labrador's Strategic Social Plan. She sits on the Social Sciences and Humanities Research Council and chairs the Audit Committee, co-chairs the Canadian Health Network and is a member of the Joint Coordinating Committee of the Voluntary Sector Initiative. She also serves on the Premier's Council on Social Development, the Capital Cost Development Alliance and Memorial University's Centre for Applied Health Research.

HUGH SEGAL is President and CEO of the Montreal-based Institute for Research on Public Policy (IRPP), Canada's oldest, non-partisan, bilingual public policy think-tank. A graduate of the University of Ottawa, he is a Senior

Fellow at the School of Policy Studies and Adjunct Professor of Public Policy at the School of Business at Queen's University. He is on the boards of the Canadian Institute for Advanced Research, the Atlantic Council, Second Cup Coffee, Vincor International, Enterprise Canada, and a member of the Finance and Audit Committee of the Toronto Hospital, and has held a series of positions in the public and private sector, including Associate Secretary of Cabinet for federal-provincial relations in Ontario, Chief of Staff to the Prime Minister of Canada, and Chair of the TACT Group of Companies.

TIMOTHY SIMBOLI is Executive Director of the Family Service Centre of Ottawa-Carleton. His educational training has focused on research in psychology and he received his doctorate from Carleton University in 1995. He has written and spoken on youth issues, program evaluation, and voluntary sector management. His work has been mainly in community-based service agencies. In his 25 years in the field, he has been the Director of a Residence for Young Offenders, the Senior Clinical Supervisor with a youth counselling organization, and the Director of Operations for the Boys and Girls Club.

JOHN STOKER is the Chief Charity Commissioner of the Charity Commission for England and Wales, a position he has held since 1999. He began his career with the Department of the Environment in 1973 and has worked mainly in the areas of housing, environment, and programs for physical and economic regeneration, apart from brief spells at the Civil Service Selection Board and Cabinet Office (Economic Secretariat) in the 1980s. From 1992 to 1996 he was Regional Director of the Government Office for Merseyside and Deputy Director General and then Director General of the National Lottery, 1997–99.

GUY TOUSIGNANT is Secretary-General of CARE International. He chairs the Steering Committee for Humanitarian Response (SCHR), an alliance of international nongovernmental organizations involved in emergency humanitarian assistance based in Geneva. He sits on the Inter-Agency Standing Committee (IASC) which brings together the UN family, the Red Cross Movement and the NGOs. He was appointed Force Commander and Assistant Secretary-General for the United Nations Assistance Mission for Rwanda in 1994. Previously he served with the Canadian Armed Forces from 1962 and was accorded seven command positions, including the National Defence College in Canada. He retired at the rank of Major-General, with the Order of the Military Merit, the Order of St-John, and the Meritorious Service Cross among other awards.

DEENA WHITE is Associate Professor of Sociology at the University of Montreal and a researcher at GRASP, a research centre for the study of social aspects of health and prevention. Her area of expertise is social policy, particularly with respect to the place of social groups as actors in policy processes, including policy development and implementation. She has conducted numerous research projects on the participation of community groups in health policies and in social assistance and workfare policies, and has published extensively in these areas. Her most recent book examines the issue of intersectoral action, with a focus on marginal groups such as the mentally ill and homeless.

MIYO YAMASHITA was data security officer for Mount Sinai Hospital in Toronto. She has worked in privacy and data security consulting since 1994. She is designing a corporate security program for Mount Sinai. She has also consulted for the pharmaceutical industry, the insurance industry, and the Canadian Bankers and Canadian Direct Marketing associations. In this capacity, Dr. Yamashita has conducted legislative impact assessments and designed legislative compliance programs and public communications strategies on Bill C-6 and other provincial privacy laws. She is currently Corporate Privacy Officer, University Health Network.

INTRODUCTION

THE IMPORTANCE OF
THE VOLUNTARY SECTOR IN
PUBLIC POLICY

Liberal Member of Parliament, Peter Milliken opened the conference by reflecting upon the importance of the voluntary sector in Canadian life. He reminded the audience, consisting largely of third sector and federal and provincial government representatives that the Liberal Party made a commitment to strengthening the voluntary sector in the 1993 election campaign. That commitment was carried forward in the most recent throne speech as well as actions that the federal government has undertaken jointly with the voluntary sector. In the face of the looming federal election, his words foreshadowed the future of the relationship between the federal government and the third sector.

In his thank you to Peter Milliken, Hugh Segal stressed the importance of thinking about the voluntary sector and its relationship to government and the private sector in a systematic and critical manner. If responsible policy decisions are to be made by the three sectors acting in concert, then we must understand their respective strengths and weaknesses and their impact upon society. Academia can play a significant role in bringing the sectors together and offering insight into how their interaction may benefit all Canadians. Theory and practice must go hand in hand to obtain the best policy results.

PETER MILLIKEN
Member of Parliament
Kingston and the Islands

I am very pleased to be here today representing the Government of Canada and the Honourable Lucienne Robillard, the Chair of the Reference Group of Ministers on the voluntary sector initiative and I am also pleased to have the chance to open this first annual conference on public policy in the third sector. This is in my constituency, but Kingston is also my home town and I have long been acquainted with the many caring Canadians whose hard work and compassion have had a significant impact on this community. The third sector is clearly extremely important in Kingston. Les Canadiens ont toujours a fait preuve d'un sens rigoureux de la responsabilité collective. C'est une caractéristique admirable. Que ce soit pour un parent, un ami, un voisin, on trouve au Canada une égale sollicitude. Notre régime de bien-être et de santé et notre système de sécurité sociale sont exemplaires. The spirit of compassion is alive and well in our country and it is indeed one of the reasons for our national prosperity. Nowhere is this compassion more evident than in the voluntary sector. The bulk of this important work takes place at the community level; however, equally important work is being undertaken by governments at all levels in partnership with leaders of the third sector from across Canada.

As a government, we have recognized that the voluntary sector represents the third pillar of our society. It is an important sector, as important as the public and private sectors. It generates key economic spinoffs and creates hundreds of thousands of jobs. It also delivers vital services in each and every community across the country. But we need to do more as a government and as a society to support organizations and the individuals they serve because they contribute to maintaining our social, economic, and cultural fabric. The Government of Canada is committed to building new relationships with Canada's third sector. That commitment was affirmed in the book, *Securing Our Future Together*. You might not remember the title, but it happened to be the jolly old "red book" for the last election campaign. And, in fact, that idea was reaffirmed in the most recent Speech from the Throne.

In his October 1999 response to the Speech from the Throne, the prime minister delineated the Liberal government strategy for the first five years of the new century and this strategy is designed to ensure that Canada starts this new era with optimism, confidence, and hope. This speech is not prepared with an election in view. The five-year strategy promotes two fundamental aspects of a successful nation: economic prosperity and quality of life. It integrates the economy, social policy, and the environment and aims to make Canada the place to be in the twenty-first century. The strategy recognizes that Canada's success as a nation has come not only from strong economic growth but from an abiding commitment to strong values. It also recognizes that the most effective approaches to strengthening quality of life are those that focus on social development and inclusion. The Government of Canada and the voluntary sector share a long history of working together to achieve mutual goals. Over the decades this relationship has shifted and changed many times and it is now transforming again.

This time, through our joint initiative, we are working together to determine how this relationship should evolve so that we can best serve Canadians. Beginning in March 1999, a very successful joint tables approach was undertaken by government and the voluntary sector to explore three key areas: (i) improving the relationship between the government and the sector; (ii) enhancing the capacity of the sector to serve Canadians; and (iii) improving the legislative and regulatory environment in which the sector operates. The joint tables proved to be a very effective model and they accomplished an extraordinary amount of work in a short time. In September of 1999, the committee released a joint report entitled, *Working Together*. This offered a wide array of innovative, far-reaching options and formed the basis for the Voluntary Sector Initiative announced in June 2000 by the Honourable Lucienne Robillard, president of the Treasury Board of Canada.

The centrepiece of the announcement was the government's reaffirmation of its commitment to work with the voluntary sector for the benefit of all Canadians. The Voluntary Sector Initiative is supported by a commitment of $90 million over the next five years. The initiative encompasses two broad objectives. The first is to help the sector increase its capacity to meet the needs of our society and the second is to work with the sector to improve the government's policies, programs and services to Canadians. This objective recognizes the sector's role in policy advice beyond service delivery. It also reflects the voluntary sector's finely attuned understanding of the needs of the people it serves. The government has made a commitment to involving the sector in policy-making that will ensure more informed policy-making by the government. But involvement in policy formulation requires the capacity to participate and a learning culture on both sides. Government departments need to incorporate the third sector more systematically and to a greater extent in the development of policy initiatives.

Good government and especially one committed to meaningful social development requires engaged citizens. Eliciting this engagement is central to the government's promise. The government seeks a meaningful, ongoing public policy dialogue between all levels of jurisdiction and the voluntary sector and indeed with all Canadian organizations and individuals. Federal ministers and officials have agreed to work with the sector leadership to advance this dialogue. We want to seek the views and opinions of the sector in these consultations as well as the views of provincial and territorial governments, business, labour, and other stakeholders. We will also want to ensure that the process embraces Canadians in urban, rural, and remote areas. As we move forward, we will count on the sector's help to find ways to broaden this process and we need to welcome and engage all those individuals and organizations who want to help shape this partnership and make it live and breathe in the communities and neighbourhoods across Canada where volunteer organizations matter most.

Our goal in this regard is that some day in the not too distant future we will look around and realize that involving the voluntary sector in policy dialogue is so entrenched that no one thinks twice about it. Program managers will involve the voluntary sector in design and implementation as a matter of course and dialogue will be the accepted way of doing business in all departments. The government knows that all three sectors (public, private, and voluntary) play equally vital roles in enhancing the quality of life of Canadians, but only in the past few years have we started to realize how independent these three sectors really are and that it is only by the three joining forces that we can truly build a stronger, healthier society.

Given the growing importance of the voluntary sector in the lives of Canadians, in part because of cutbacks in government, and the increasing interest of government, academia, and other segments of Canadian society in this most relevant area of study, I would like to congratulate the School of Policy Studies at Queen's University on the launch of this first annual conference on Public Policy and the Third Sector. I hope that the collaboration between the School and the government's voluntary sector initiative will continue to expand and deepen our understanding of the benefits of such collaboration and that these benefits can move forward with our collective agenda of engaging the third sector in informed discussion, sound policy development, and effective action.

I am particularly pleased to have the opportunity to welcome you to Kingston and to Queen's and on behalf of the Government of Canada I wish you every success at this conference. I hope that the results of it are very helpful in this dialogue that we are hoping to develop in a major way and that this can be a starting point for that development. Thank you very much for attending and I hope you enjoy the conference.

HUGH SEGAL
President
Institute for Research on Public Policy

I would like to thank our local member of parliament, Peter Milliken, "Monsieur Milliken est un être qui faire des choses au valeur dans de la communité ici à Kingston et qui travaille beaucoup et fort pour nos organisations. Peter est toujours ici à Kingston. Peter le prochain matin le commencez à Ottawa de nouveau. He is a person — I say this, at least for the next 48 hours in a completely nonpartisan way and mean it — who has always been there for the voluntary sector in this community without regard to partisanship. He has been there to sometimes push government to reflect just a tiny bit on the immense value of a local initiative which might not have been recognized as quickly without the aid, assistance, and counsel of the local member of parliament. He really has been an outstanding friend to the School and I wish him every possible success.

Your presence here today and the fact that registration closed a week early because of the tremendous demand to be here speaks to something that I think is truly exciting and that is the emergence of public policy around the not-for-profit sector as a new and compelling stream of what we used to call public life and public administration. It is, I think, reflective of the fact that the innate sense we have all had, as Canadians, of the value of this sector and its importance as a catalyst for what is most important in our communities and what defines the quality of life and civility that we share. It is something that can no longer be left unstudied in the context of what it means for public policy and what public policy means for it. If we do not put the same level of concern and intellectual capacity behind the issues in this sector as we do behind private sector issues and behind public policy questions in the purest sense, we will all, as a society, suffer as a result. We will be diminished. We will lose one of the great strengths that we know this community reflects.

There are some really fascinating questions that will be dealt with in some measure by this conference. They are, however, too large for any one conference or group of commentators, academics, practitioners, and specialists to address in any one time. Do our state institutions embrace in reality and spirit the dynamics and exigencies of the third sector? If ministers and politicians, the federal and provincial level of all political affiliations, say one thing but the Canada Customs and Revenue Agency says another in their regulations, what does that mean? Do the elements of our political culture truly encourage a dynamic and competitive third sector or are there built into our political culture some normative constraints that say we only want the third sector to go so far? We do not want them in some areas, we want them in a neat categorized position, and if this is so, why?

When the third sector does work in partnership with the state, the dynamic partnership to which Peter referred, who is the master? Whose values prevail? Are they the values of the state agency, duly constituted, appropriately accountable, with all that that represents in a democracy such as ours? Or are they the values of the third sector organizations that may have been coming at things in a very different way, with a very different perspective that does not conform to the orthodoxy of public policy but was nevertheless meeting a specific need that might not have been met through the current public policy approach. Are there better ways to manage the regulatory process so as to maximize the sector's contribution? Are we doing things in our public policy framework as it exists today for the third sector that are in fact unwittingly working against the capacity of the sector to meet its goals and fill the gaps it has to fill? Why do we make charitable status in this country tougher to attain than in many of our OECD partners and certainly far tougher to attain than in our partner and neighbour to the south? How do we ensure that the voluntary sector's progress does not happen at the expense of legitimate and appropriate public sector responsibilities? How do we ensure that the voluntary sector with its strengths and weaknesses is not asked to take upon itself burdens and responsibilities that are normally the discourse of public administration? How do we work with the many federal and provincial policy and regulatory anomalies where different messages are sent, again unwittingly by virtue of how this country is organized?

There is a lot to discuss and while those who are part of our panels will bring some thoughtful and important perspectives and experiences, the truth of the matter is that this is an area where reality on the ground is changing every day. The marketplace of ideas around this phenomenon should reflect those changes. Your presence here as participants who are involved in various aspects and at different levels is vital in order for us to generate the insights that will advance the understanding of the sector, better inform public policy practitioners and decisionmakers and allow us to move forward in a constructive way.

PANEL ONE

IMPROVING THE RELATIONSHIP BETWEEN THE THIRD SECTOR AND THE CANADIAN STATE

ARTHUR DRACHE, QC
Drache, Burke-Robertson & Buchmayer

A Charity Tribunal for Canada?

Let me tell you what the problems are from my point of view as a lawyer. I am one of the few lawyers in Canada who practises almost exclusively charities and nonprofit law. I would say, if use is a benchmark, 50 percent of the time there might be five of us in the country. Now a lot of lawyers do some charities and nonprofit law, but there are very few of us who put in a majority of time. I have been doing this since 1976 when I left the Department of Finance. When I was in the department I drafted the tax legislation relating to charities so I have seen the charities law from the point of view of a bureaucrat. I did the draft of the tax legislation and so on. I have been a practitioner and I have been a teacher as well.

The situation, as I see it, and as it has developed within about the past five years is that we have a serious crisis from a legal point of view with regard to charities; and that also represents a policy crisis. Usually when we talk about change, and I have tried to talk about the concept of a charities tribunal for Canada, the first thing people say is "if it ain't broke don't fix it." Well, I want to tell you that indeed, "it's broke." It is broken so badly that only radical surgery can change it. Let me go back to where we started. We, the lawyers, because I think it fair to say that it was the lawyers and some of their key clients who started pushing this process because we got to the point where we could not operate satisfactorily anymore.

The start of reform is a question of definition. What is a charity? Now, as many of you will be well aware, that broad general issue flows from English common law. The usual starting point is the *Statute of Elizabeth 1601*. This is continually quoted by the courts today as authority. Of course, the *Statute of Elizabeth* came from the ballad of *Piers Ploughman* which was written in the fourteenth century, but that is another matter. If you take a look at the *Piers Ploughman* you will find it almost exactly a moot pickup of the activities in the fourteenth century and move it to the start of the seventeenth century and that is what our courts are using today.

The situation was not that bad into the mid-1980s for the simple reason that the government was spending money widely within the sector. As long as the sector and its components were getting government money, the question of whether they were or were not charities became very much a secondary function. For example, a particular department — in those days the Secretary of State, but now the Department of Canadian Heritage — charged with multiculturalism gave money to multicultural organizations. That was one of their client bases. They gave money to women's organizations. They gave money to organizations promoting patriotism. They also gave out flags. They had a wide and diverse client base. What happened is the money started drying up about 1985 and the logical thing was to do one of two things: roll over and die like the Canadian Crafts Council which no longer exists or go out and start raising money. The first thing that happens is that you say, "Well if we want to raise money, we have got to be registered as a charity." And lo and behold they suddenly discover that they cannot be registered as a charity. If you have a situation in which the courts are looking to English law of 1601, how much multiculturalism did you have in England in 1601? This is what we are looking at. Incidentally, Scotland is now looking at new definitions of charities because they do not like the English definition. They want a "made in Scotland" definition.

I am not really oversimplifying it. This is exactly what happened as it was discovered that you cannot register something as a promotion of multiculturalism. You cannot register something that is a promotion of patriotism. You can only register an environmental charity if it is a hands-on charity. If you go out and pick up garbage as part of your charitable function, that is okay. But, for instance, to talk about promoting good environmental practices is not charitable. And there is a long list. A neighbourhood organization to look after needs in the neighbourhood is held not to be charitable; organizations to promote better international understanding and tolerance are held not to be charitable; legal aid for poor people and legal aid clinics are held not to be charitable, each of these organizations face this trauma once. I am a lawyer and I see the trauma all the time. I am the one who has to say to them, "Look you guys are doing great things and if the world were a logical, rational place, you would be registered as a charity." But it is not. Promoting racial tolerance is not charitable. Okay? Promoting the integration of immigrants into our society, the Supreme Court of Canada specifically said it was not charitable.

I cannot change the common law. Changing the common law is essentially almost by definition an impossibility. What I want to do is change the law where it counts. I want to change it for income tax purposes. That is all. I do not want to mess around with 400 years of common law. You love it, you can keep it. You know, the Ontario Law Reform Commission thought it was wonderful. They would not touch a word of the common law. Fine. Keep it. But I want to have a definition for practical purposes and practical means income purposes. I want it changed.

In England, the Charity Commission has changed a great deal. For example, in something such as promotion of racial tolerance, the commission worked out the logic — not by going back to the Statute of 1601 — but as policy. Racial tolerance is a policy, racial hatred is a crime, all major parties in Parliament agree that there is a consensus in the community, therefore we will register this type of organization. Even there they changed. When they ran into a tough case that dealt with amateur sports (because the promotion of amateur sports is not charitable) they changed the law. They said, "such and such activity is deemed to be and always has been charitable," thus wiping out 200 years of law. In Canada, we developed it with regard to that law. The Canadian Amateur Athletic Association was registered for the sole purpose of getting private funding for athletes for the Montreal Olympics. There is a view that Canada did not do well in Australia. I point out that in 1976 this was the only home country that did not win a gold medal. I do not suggest that it was a result of the federal government's policy but it was not particularly helpful in that regard. Greg Joy, who won a silver medal, is now a proud member of the voluntary sector community in Ottawa.

So there is a problem of definition. My own view, and the view that I put forward, is that either we legislate a definition or we legislate a list. Peter Milliken made reference to the joint-tables process. I thought the process was not spectacular, but the joint-table members suggested that Canadians would support the following list, organizations that promote: tolerance and understanding within the community of groups enumerated in the Canadian Human Rights Code; the provisions of international conventions to which Canada has subscribed; tolerance and understanding between people of the various nations; the culture, language, and heritage of Canadians with origins in other countries;

the dissemination of information about environmental issues and sustainable development; and volunteerism and philanthropy. Of course, they stayed away from such emotionally charged things as promoting patriotism. That, of course, is definitely a "no-no" in this country. If you want to set up an organization to further better understanding between French and English you cannot do it. That is not charitable. Now, when the due process started, this was dropped. This is not on the agenda.

Let me turn to the next step. I think that a definition is needed. The alternative (though I consider it to be not as good an alternative but an alternative) would be to create a new body to come up with a definition. In a paper that I wrote with Laird Hunter, a lawyer who with me argued the Vancouver Immigrant Women's Society case before the Supreme Court of Canada, we decided to use the term tribunal because we did not want the baggage of the Charity Commission. We are not trying to replicate it in Canada. For starters, we have federal-provincial jurisdictions to contend with and secondly, we do not think that we can play around with the common law quite the way that the Charity Commission can. But the problem, and this is a problem all over the world, is that as long as the issue of what is a charity for tax purposes — for tax purposes only — is left to the tax authorities, the wrong people are making the decisions. For instance, a new client brought me a letter that had been dated 4 July 2000. The letter threatens deregistration of the charity based on an audit that took place in 1996. It took four and a half years for them to report on the audit. There is nobody in the organization who even knows what it was about because there were only two people in the organization and they both left. They have an auditor threatening them after four and a half years. Another example involved the government response to a request that we had filed to allow a charity to change its fiscal year-end (a very simple and routine matter). This had been granted. The letter was dated August and as is so often the case in letters from the Canada Custom and Revenue Agency (CCRA) the letter began, "we regret the delay in responding to you." The delay was 14 months.

The third example began with a phone call from a friend of mine, a lawyer doing a voluntary job, charity, routine, small thing, *pro bono*. This is a person used to dealing with CCRA and taxes. He had sent a letter in September to CCRA requesting registration for a charity. The reply letter came three weeks later and said, "Thank you very much. It will be assigned to an assessor in March or April." Not dealt with but would be assigned to somebody in March or April! The CCRA is without doubt the most efficient organization in all other ways. If you file your tax return, on paper or electronically, half the time you receive your refund (if your planning is so bad that you get a refund) in four or five weeks. But in the charities directorate, it takes them six months to assign the file! Incidentally, the *Income Tax Act* says that if you have not heard within 180 days of sending in your application, you are deemed to have been refused. Okay? The thing is not going to be assigned to somebody when the Act says you have been deemed to have been refused! If it were not for the fact that the appeal procedure is so outrageous, there would be more appeals. I did a check in my office alone. I could have 27 appeals at the Court of Appeal on cases now deemed to have been refused on the grounds that they have received no answer.

This is without a doubt the most hopeless organization in the government. I said that to the last director, and when he left he told somebody that at "least he is glad to be moving to another part of the department so that he doesn't have to hear Drache call him by name." This is not new. When they get a new director I am sure he will say, "We are going to fix it up."

Well, I have been watching this thing for 15 years and it has gotten worse and worse, and now it is terrible. The fact of the matter is — let me cut to the heart of it — they talk about "if it ain't broke, don't fix it." There are two things that are broken. First, all over the world, people are taking a look at the question of whether from a policy point of view the tax authority should be making this decision. What you have is the fox guarding the hen house: the tax people are the ones who make the decision about who is going to get a tax break. Not the law, but the tax department. Second, they are not trained in charities law and they do not have any social reason to be involved in this. They are not even lawyers in most cases. They are not involved in the voluntary sector and yet these are the people who make "life and death" decisions for organizations. The appeal procedure is virtually impossible because it starts at the federal Court of Appeal. No one can afford it. In principle, I take the position that the tax authorities are not the people to be making the decisions. This is principle and policy. In practical terms, the CCRA charities directorate is so bad that it cannot be fixed. Something completely new is needed. Ideally, in my view, it would be legislation. The *Income Tax Act* would contain a list or a definition, and a new body to deal with the charities. But if the status quo is to remain and CCRA keeps the directorate at least there should be a new set of rules that say:, "These are the tests set by Parliament."

My voice is not alone. In the Vancouver Immigrant Women case, Iaccobucci writing for the majority, said, in effect, that "we need to look again at what is meant by the term charity at least within the Income Tax Act.... It is for Parliament, not the courts to make that decision." This is the only time the Supreme Court has exercised judicial restraint in the past 15 years and he does it to my case! He liked everything we said, he just was not going to change anything." But the fact of the matter is that there is a consensus among everybody involved, except those who are defending turf, that change is necessary.

The two things on which the Voluntary Sector Initiative is specifically or non-specifically silent are the issue of definition and the issue of tribunal. I think that what it really means is that on the hard points, the hard stuff not this fluffy stuff about contracts and compacts and agreements between government and the sector, they are afraid to get involved. I am sure there are other points of view on that.

PATRICK MONAHAN
Professor
Osgoode Hall Law School

Redesigning the Regulatory Framework

Let me just say by way of introduction that there is a saying that when you get a number of economists in a room, the number of opinions will at least equal that number. I think the same could probably be said of most lawyers, although that often depends on who their clients are. In this case, I am going to take a slightly different view than the view that was put forward by Arthur Drache, though I agree with many of the points that he made in terms of the need for reform in this area. I think, however, we do part company on some of the proposals.

Let me say as well that I have come to this issue recently. About a year and a half ago I was approached by the Kahanoff Foundation to consider proposals for institutional reform and regulatory reform in this area. After protesting that I knew nothing about the subject, I was informed that in this case this was an advantage: I had no preconceived notions or turf to defend. I could not be accused of advancing a predetermined agenda. I agreed to prepare a study of the need for regulatory reform and this led to the book I co-authored with Elie Roth entitled *Federal Regulation of Charities*.

There are many well-known criticisms of the federal process for regulating charities. The criticisms suggest that the Canada Customs and Revenue Agency (CCRA) is unduly restrictive and/or even arbitrary in its determination of whether to register an entity as a charitable organization. It is also said that the process is too secretive and lacks transparency; concerns over privacy in the *Income Tax Act* mean that we are not able to access, nor do the government and departments publicize, applications that are denied and there are no reasons given generally regarding registration. Although a letter denying the application may be given to the organization, it is not published. Since it is not part of the public record, we have no way generally of tracking CCRA registration decisions.

The legal definition of charity is based on the Pemsel test which is the House of Lords decision in the 1890s that relied on the 1601 statute, the *Statute of Elizabeth*. The categories of charity that were set out in this 1893 House of Lords case, formed the basis of the common law definition of charity. There is no definition of charity in the *Income Tax Act*.

The appeal process for a decision on registration, as Arthur Drache pointed out, involves an appeal to the federal Court of Appeal, which is extremely costly. It requires the individual to retain counsel and is a relatively long process. Therefore, it is inaccessible to most organizations and there is very little ongoing review or supervision of CCRA decisions by the courts.

To what extent are charities regulated on an ongoing basis once they are registered? The process really stops to a large extent at the decision to register. There is an audit function that is performed by an organization called Consulting and Audit Canada, which is a separate entity that audits about 0.6 percent of charities annually, but there is relatively little ongoing regulation once the CCRA makes its decision.

It is said that the courts are ill-equipped to make social policy. This point is often debated in terms of the role of courts but the key argument is that the decisions on which charities to register are social policy decisions the courts are not equipped to make and should not be making. It is often argued that those decisions should be made by Parliament or by elected representatives. It is also commonly argued that the current restriction on charities engaging in political activities is questionable. The current restrictions are that political activities must be ancillary and incidental to the activities and purpose of a charitable organization. There is a limit, in fact, on the amount of money that can be expended annually by charities on political activities. These problems are said to be so fundamental that they need to be resolved by legislative and institutional reform, creating some kind of organization outside the CCRA such as a voluntary sector commission with decision-making powers on registrations. There have also been calls for greater transparency in the registration process, reforming the appeals process, and introducing intermediate sanctions given that the only sanction that the CCRA now has is to deregister a charity.

This is generally regarded as draconian since if you fail to file a form on time, the sanction is deregistration.

Well, what is the current situation? We need to step back and look at the present situation before we decide what needs to be reformed. Currently we have about 80,000 registered charities. There were about 78,000 registered charities in April 1999 and the number of charities is growing so 80,000 is my estimate of the current situation. Each year there are about 4,000 to 5,000 applications for new registrations and of those approximately three of four or 75 percent are approved by the CCRA. I conducted interviews with individuals in the CCRA or as it was then known, Revenue Canada Charities Division, about what actually happens to the other 25 percent. It turns out that there are only about 100 applicants who are formally denied charitable status each year. They receive letters saying "your application is denied." In the other cases, applicants are given what is called an "administrative fairness letter" whereby certain questions are raised about the application by CCRA, questions about the nature of the application, whether in fact it meets the criteria for charity and for registration purposes. In the majority of those cases, the application is abandoned. Now, we do not know why that happens nor have I any data on what happens then. It is possible that the organization refashions an application and puts it forward in a somewhat different form. Only a very small number of requests are actually formally refused.

It is important to have a baseline of comparison when examining proposals for reform. We need to compare ourselves, then, to other countries that have political, economic, and legal systems that are most similar to Canada's, namely the United States, the United Kingdom, Western European countries, Australia, and New Zealand. Many of these are common-law jurisdictions and many share a common legal culture and legal system. They also have economies and political structures that are broadly similar to Canada's.

When we look at these jurisdictions, we note one thing that is generally the case across all of them: they all draw a fundamental distinction between an organization that is tax exempt (it does not pay tax on its income) as opposed to an organization to which tax-deductible donations can be made. In Canada, until 1988 we had a system where the taxpayer received a deduction for a donation to a charity. That was converted into a tax credit, which is the current system, so that donors receive a credit on their taxes which then comes back to them when they file their tax return. What we typically find, both in Canada and elsewhere, is that the former category of tax-exempt organizations is broader than the latter category of organizations that are entitled to grant a tax deduction or tax credit to donors. For example, in Canada, we have about 80,000 charities but we have an additional 100,000 nonprofit agencies and, as the Panel on Accountability and Governance in the Voluntary Sector Report pointed out, the voluntary sector is in fact far broader than just registered charities.

We might ask ourselves, why is it, that all of these legal systems define the category of organization that provides tax benefits to donors more narrowly than those that are merely tax exempt? The answer is obvious. It is because in the case where a benefit is granted to the donor, it is not simply the donor who is giving money, it is also the taxpayer or the fiscal system. My Osgoode Hall colleague, Neil Brooks, one of Canada's leading tax authorities, illustrates the point with a simple example. If a taxpayer donates $1,000 to a charity, he or she gets a tax credit worth approximately $500. Neil says that what is happening here is that the taxpayer is giving $500 of his or her own money while at the same time enlisting the Treasury to give $500 of the Treasury's money. In fact, there are two grants being made, through the system of a public contribution to the charitable organization.

We should also notice that this system is quite different from a system of grants where the government gives direct grants. Under that system the government has to reveal who received the grants. In the past the government tended to give direct grants to a number of nongovernmental lobby groups and that provoked a lot of criticism. Canadians questioned whether we should really be giving these direct grants. At least in that situation everybody could tell at the end of the year how much money was going to which organization. But, of course, in a system where grants come in the form of tax credits, you do not have that at the end of the year. We do not have an accounting of how much was contributed to which organization because the priorities are determined not by the government or by Parliament but by the actions of the individuals donating money. Some would say that it is a good thing because it is grassroots democracy. However, we have to recognize that not only are these individuals donating that money, they are also enlisting the Treasury in that contribution. So, therefore, it is not just the recipient organizations that have an interest in making sure that the government adheres to rule of law and fundamental principles in administering the system of charitable registration. The taxpayer, too, has an interest. He or she needs to know, ought to know and has a right to know how, and on what basis, these decisions are being made.

When comparing Canada to other industrialized democracies, it would be my judgement that the quantum of tax assistance provided by Canada to charitable groups is relatively generous by international standards. It has become more generous in recent years, since, for example, a taxpayer can now receive credit for donations of up to 75 percent of income. Prior to 1995, the limit was only 20 percent of income. In 1996, it went to 50 percent of income. More recently, the limit has gone up to 75 percent. That compares to a current limit of 50 percent of income in the United States. In Canada the tax expenditure (or government revenue foregone) on charitable donations and the charitable tax credit is about $1.5 billion annually which is an increase of about 50 percent from what it was in 1995. I point this out not to criticize this rise but simply to point out that relatively speaking we have made moves in the last couple of years to make Canada relatively generous by these standards.

Now, in terms of the definition of charity most of the jurisdictions alluded to above define the entities that can provide tax assistance to donors by reference to these same Pemsel categories as Canada uses. There have been numerous calls throughout the twentieth century in England, the United States, and elsewhere for the need to reform. They have been calling for a statutory definition of charity for over 50 years in England. Reports have asked, "How can we possibly have this 1601 statute coming through this 1893 House of Lords decision? It is archaic. We will have to have a statutory definition." But these proposals have never been implemented. These jurisdictions have never succeeded in settling on a statutory definition of charity and have all ultimately lived with the existing definition. It is also the case that the political purposes doctrine is widely accepted. Most jurisdictions impose restrictions on charities engaging in political activities. These restrictions may not be exactly what we have in Canada but most say that a charity should not be engaged in political purposes or in political activities. It should be engaged in charitable activities. Engagement in political activities should only be allowed to the extent that they are ancillary to the charitable activities. Of course, this is broadly the rule that we have here in Canada.

Again, in terms of regulatory oversight, the general rule — with the exception of England where there is a Charity Commission that makes decisions on the registration of charities — is that the tax authority administers the system of tax registration. In the US this is the general rule, and in Australia, there has recently been a major reform of the system of charitable oversight but they have not moved away from the general rule. All of these jurisdictions have a limited number of appeals from denials of registration. This is a general phenomenon, not just found in Canada. As well, we would say that other than Ontario and Alberta, in Canada there is little regulatory oversight of charitable organizations on an ongoing basis, unlike in England where the Charity

Commission does exercise an ongoing oversight function. Why does this difference exist? In Canada, jurisdiction over charities is actually provincial according to a specific provision in the 1867 *Constitution Act*. This means that the federal government has very limited jurisdiction over charities. Most of the provinces, however, have not actually exercised their jurisdiction, other than Alberta and Ontario.

What conclusions do I draw from this consideration of our current situation and from these international comparisons? It seems to me that the case for greater transparency in the registration process is clear and compelling. If there is no transparency, if you do not know how and why decisions are made, then ultimately a system exists that is prone to arbitrariness, not because the people involved are arbitrary but because they do not have a system of regular public scrutiny applied to their decisions. What was remarkable to me in my discussions with various officials was that I would say, "Well, I understand that this type of organization is not regularly granted charitable status." And the answer would come back, "No, no, we have granted charitable status to organizations like that." There did not seem to be, in other words, the needed transparency in the decision-making. Clearly there needs to be some regular and systematic public reporting of decisions on applications for registration.

Calls for transparency give rise to concerns about confidentiality, but it seems to me that those can be met in a variety of ways. One possibility is to address these concerns in the same way that the CCRA currently deals with advanced tax rulings. When you ask for an advanced tax ruling, you have to submit two versions of the application. You submit the version to the department that will be confidential and then you submit the version that will be published. Thus, this could be the process for charitable organizations: they would provide an application and a version of the application suitable for publication that would delete any identifying or confidential information. We would still have an opportunity for public scrutiny of that decision. There also needs to be a system of internal administrative appeals that is similar to that for individual as well as corporate taxpayers. There should also be an appeal to the tax court where there is greater informality than the federal Court of Appeals.

On the other hand, in my view, the case for enacting a statutory definition is not nearly as clear and compelling. The international comparisons, in fact, bear that out. The existing definition used in other countries is broadly similar to the one used in Canada, although there are differences at the margins. The common-law methodology, which is a methodology of reasoning by analogy, provides flexibility and the capacity to respond to changing circumstances. It seems to me that the fact that these different jurisdictions with so many varied circumstances have been able to live with the categories from the Pemsel case demonstrate that these categories are sufficiently flexible that they can be adapted to circumstances as needed. It also seems to me that there is some need for clarifying what the definition of political purposes is, although I do not think we should abolish the political purposes doctrine. I think it is a sound doctrine as evidenced by its acceptance in other jurisdictions.

In terms of institutional reform, the case for devolving the registration function outside the CCRA is not a strong one. It would be stronger if we were going to create a body that would have more effective regulatory oversight of the sector as a whole, not just the matter of registering charities. But the difficulty is that charitable regulation is within provincial jurisdiction rather than federal. If a charity commission were to be effective, then the provinces would have to be involved. There is little likelihood of that kind of consensus emerging from the provinces. The case for a commission to deal with just registrations is not strong.

In conclusion, there is a need for significant reform in this sector. However, in my view, reform needs to be incremental and built on existing institutions rather than on creating entirely new ones.

SUSAN FLETCHER
Executive Director
Voluntary Sector Task Force, Privy Council Office

The Voluntary Sector Initiative: The Government Perspective

The Liberal Party talked about deepening its engagement with the voluntary sector in its 1997 election platform, the "Red Book." This included a vision for the voluntary sector as the third pillar of Canadian society. When the Liberals came to power, the Red Book vision became the policy of the Government of Canada and federal officials started to look at what the vision actually meant in practice.

The timing was right. There was growing global recognition about the importance of volunteers and the voluntary sector for civil society. The sector itself was questioning its relationship with governments and had commissioned

Ed Broadbent to lead a review of the issues related to its accountability and governance. Several provinces were undertaking processes to improve their relations with the voluntary sector. These, plus a recognition by the Government of Canada of the importance of the voluntary sector to government programming, suggested that the time was right to try to develop a relationship at the cross-governmental level with the voluntary sector.

In the Spring of 1999, ministers agreed that officials could engage in a new kind of consultation process with the voluntary sector. Public servants were encouraged to open a dialogue with senior leaders of the voluntary sector and talk about problems that we should be trying to solve together. We called these "joint-table" processes. The processes had two objectives: to serve as models for working together and to identify the priority issues. We looked at priorities in three different areas: (i) examining the relationship itself; (ii) strengthening the capacity of the voluntary sector and the government to work together; and (iii) improving the regulatory or legal framework within which the sector works.

Both Government of Canada officials and voluntary sector leaders brought impressive amounts of knowledge and experience to the table. Everybody recognized the value of the others' contributions. But the task of identifying the most important issues to target was not an easy one. Twenty-six issues were included in a report entitled *Working Together*, which was made public in September 1999. Government ministers responded positively to the report and its proposals.

The 1999 Speech from the Throne reiterated the government's commitment to the voluntary sector. Its importance was further reinforced when the prime minister created, in February 2000, a group of nine ministers to provide stewardship (rather than a single minister which was the more common practice).

The Voluntary Sector Initiative (VSI), with funding of $94.6 million over five years, was launched in June 2000. The VSI has two policy objectives: to increase the capacity of the sector to meet the demands that society places on it and to further develop the relationship. Part of the second objective is to help the government do its business better by involving the sector not only as a service deliverer but also as a key informant in our policy and program development.

The three original priority areas have been continued as themes in the initiative. In the relationship-building theme, government officials will work closely with the sector leaders to develop an accord. The accord will examine how we work together, what our mutual expectations are, and what the values and principles underpinning the relationship should be. (On 5 December 2001, the

Government of Canada and the voluntary sector formalized their relationship.) In addition to the accord document, a plan will be developed to implement and report on the success of our relationship building. A joint coordinating committee will provide oversight to the initiative generally.

Within the government, the Voluntary Sector Task Force will coordinate the government's work. There is also money available to the sector for a secretariat to coordinate their work and enhance the engagement of the voluntary sector organizations in the initiative. While the initiative focuses on cross-governmental relationships, resources have also been set aside to involve the voluntary sector in the development of departmental policies. The view was that success would depend on individual departments broadening their policy relationships with voluntary sector organizations. Funds will be used by departments to enhance the capacity of their sector partners to contribute to the policy process.

The second theme is strengthening the voluntary sector's capacity, which includes information collection, analysis, and dissemination; the development of a research agenda; and human resource planning and strategies to help the sector to be more effective in what it does. Money has also been set aside to assist the sector in the use of information technology, to move beyond VOLNET which helps connect the voluntary sector to itself and to others, and to create content and an interactive possibility for the sector. Other capacity issues to be addressed are the promotion of volunteering and the creation of awareness about the voluntary sector's social and economic contribution to Canadian society

Third, we are looking at federal government funding and regulatory practices. The federal government contributes to voluntary sector financing through tax expenditures under the *Income Tax Act*, and through the direct funding of organizations by departments using grants and contributions or contracts. Issues in delivering direct funding will be reviewed, and barriers will be identified and hopefully eliminated. Regulatory questions such as the appeal process, sanctions, and reporting requirements will be examined.

We are still at the early stages. The work of the VSI is being conducted in a collaborative manner and will focus on information development and dissemination, research on best practices, and broad consultations across the country.

These broad consultations will focus on the sector but will also include other key players in Canadian society. Certainly from the Government of Canada's point of view, it will be important to hear from the provinces and territories, private sector, academia, and labour organizations.

We can expect many challenges as we move forward. The very concept of partnership can lead to expectations by sector partners about their involvement in all decision-making processes. While the VSI promotes a collaborative governance model, the democratic institutions in the federal government have been set up to ensure the freedom of ministers to make decisions in the best interest of all Canadians. The role and accountabilities of public servants means that while the policy process can be collaborative, political decision-making can not. Moreover, the Government of Canada operates with an inherently hierarchical structure. Managing a horizontal file (involving many departments) in this context, further challenges decision-making clarity. Finally, the cultures of the government and voluntary sector are very different not only in what we do but how we do it.

To me, we will have achieved success if together we have created an environment where we can learn together, where we can understand and value each other, and hopefully where we can achieve some results.

SUSAN CARTER
Executive Director
Voluntary Sector Initiative Secretariat

Building an Asymmetrical Relationship: The Federal Government and Voluntary Sector

In a number of aspects, the federal government and the voluntary sector have important differences that can create uncertainty and often frustration when it comes to working together. Because of these differences, the asymmetries that government and the voluntary sector exhibit pose challenges in developing common ground for understanding and for all aspects of the work itself. From my vantage point I would like to share what I am observing as some of the major challenges posed by these asymmetries and suggest where common ground might be found.

The federal public service is bound together by ties such as common personnel practices that have no equivalent in the voluntary sector. The federal public service is just that — a service where certain norms of process and procedure apply. In the voluntary sector, those from networks such as the United Way or the YMCAs may have a shared context, in some cases even a distinct language, but beyond that the approaches of one organization have no connections with another. In practical terms this means that when people from government and the voluntary sector are around a table together, those from the voluntary sector are going to have to find common ground with one another in addition to finding common ground with their government counterparts.

A second area of difference is structure and more specifically, the presence of hierarchy in one sector and not in the other. There is an overall hierarchy to the federal government that has implications for both decision-making and for issues of representation. Within the government, proposals and recommendations ultimately move upward and decisions come down. Since the voluntary sector has no overall upstairs, proposals and recommendations are more likely to move outward, seeking concurrence or support on some or all of the proposed direction. As a result, decision-making within a particular voluntary organization can be breathtakingly fast compared to that in government departments. But decision-making across the sector as a whole can often take what feels like a lifetime.

The absence of a single hierarchy in the voluntary sector has implications for who speaks for the sector. Voice derives much more from strength of numbers, from the consensus of large numbers within the sector who have agreed to have these positions taken forward and tend to be very issue-specific. Positions within the voluntary sector derive much more from a base of expertise or moral authority than from representation. In the public service, voice tends to come as a function of the hierarchy with positions based on agreed or adopted policies. Public servants generally speak for their department within clearly agreed parameters that either have been cleared in advance or have been previously articulated by someone more senior.

A further area of asymmetry has to do with time and continuity. Many in the voluntary sector have been involved in these issues for a considerable time whereas the government members tend to be newer. While both in this case can be extremely valuable, there can be a lot of frustration and misunderstandings. The negative or helpful policies of one administration constitute the context that the voluntary sector is operating in when it next sits down with government and it also sets the tone for how the sector is likely to approach these issues.

Lastly, the imbalance of financial resources (between the third sector and government) introduces inequalities in the power relationship and in the interaction that underlies much of the dealings between the two organizations. Despite the efforts within partnerships to recognize the problems, it is very challenging to get beyond the asker and dispenser mode. The voluntary organizations often feel required to approach government under a banner that says "we promise not to discuss money" while government officials often expect that every turn in the discussion is leading toward a pitch (for more money).

Given these fairly significant underlying differences and asymmetries, what are some of the ways in which common ground could be developed? First, both partners need to overcome the tendency to look for reflections of their own structures and of their own way of doing things when dealing with the other. In other words, rather than seeing some of these asymmetries as obstacles or problems, they should be viewed as potential for different kinds of decision-making and dialogue. Also, the open and collaborative decision-making that might be embraced or promoted widely within the voluntary sector is never going to be fully possible within the federal or any level of government. A second approach would be to move toward a relationship that is based on a recognition of what each sector has to offer so that while one party has access to financial resources, the other has knowledge and expertise based on years of wrestling with tough problems and finding improvements in communities across the country as well as a recognition that both are essential and based on public trust.

Public trust is critical to both. Government is entrusted with taxpayers' dollars and the way that these are spent, but the voluntary sector for its part is also entrusted with dollars and with the faith and trust of all those who rely on what it delivers. Each side can benefit from what the other has to offer.

The second ground is to translate this into what can be built when these two sectors recognize each other and move toward another point. Venture capitalists, for example, do not look for money on the table from the companies they fund. They look for ideas and the ability to execute these ideas. There is an incredible opportunity to change the existing pattern of the relationship and to build on this change based on mutual respect and understanding. As part of the underpinnings of the Voluntary Sector Initiative it is something we can be looking toward.

SELECTED COMMENTS FROM THE DISCUSSION

SUSAN PHILLIPS
School of Public Administration
Carleton University

I would like to connect the need to expand access to the tax system with the themes of community-building and the voluntary sector initiative. We are making a fundamental mistake about policy discourse if we see expanding the definition of, or expanding access to the tax system as a regulatory issue. It is fundamentally an issue about capacity-building. If we are asking the sector to do more to help communities help themselves, then you have to give them the policy tools. As Arthur Drache pointed out, one of the critical policy tools is providing incentives for people to give. Part of my concern has been the fact that we formed the definition as a regulatory issue and then put it aside. One might ask the question, why hasn't this moved forward? And some of us might be suspicious, not the revenue people, but that other great bastion of social policy-making in this country, the Department of Finance. I recall sitting in Paul Martin's office on the day of the release of the Broadbent Panel on Accountability and Governance in the Voluntary Sector. Ed Broadbent tried to convince the minister about the need to have greater access to the tax system and made the case that people in the sector were very conservative: they were not going to let wild groups into the Sector. At that time, Martin made at least an implicit commitment that the Department of Finance would do costing around this. Concerns are wildly overstated or overestimated, in my view, that if you expand the definition of charity you increase tax expenditures. Has the Department of Finance done that kind of costing and is it, in fact, a stumbling block to getting the issue of access to the tax system back on the agenda?

[Editor's note: the costing is being undertaken as part of the federal government's funding study of the voluntary sector.]

FRASER VALENTINE
Department of Political Science
University of Toronto

As we all know, a whole series of non-constitutional changes involving program review, the social union framework agreement, and the Canada Health and Social Transfer, have in many ways altered the relationship among the provinces and between the provinces and the federal government. Those changes have had a significant and profound impact on the voluntary sector and on certain segments of the sector more than others, which leads to asymmetry. My work is on disability rights organizations and persons with disabilities themselves. These changes have had significant and negative impacts on those organizations and persons. Thus, my question pertains to the Voluntary Sector Initiative at the federal level. Where do the provinces fit into this initiative, especially given that health, welfare, and education are significant policy areas for the sector itself? I understand that the provinces are going to be involved, but we all know that they need to be involved in a very concrete way.

ARTHUR DRACHE

One point I should make about the issue of definition of charity is that the provinces have already indicated that they were not going to be bound anymore by the federal definition. They seem to have their own income tax acts, but they were also going to develop their own tests because they were so dissatisfied with the federal process. As far as I can tell, they have not done it. Right now in order to get a charity registered for provincial purposes, it is necessary to show that it is registered for federal services. You can register the charity federally, then when you go back you give that information and they rubber stamp it. But they have indicated that they are not happy with this, they are not happy with the federal government, and they are becoming more and more rude. One of the things that is developing is a change in the provincial tax systems and within that context what you could have, is provinces redefining what is a charity, at the very least for provincial tax purposes. There is a possibility then of having a dual definition. There is now essentially a dual definition in Ontario now because what is considered to be charitable by the Public Trustee of Ontario for Ontario law is quite often out of step with what is considered to be charitable by the federal tax systems. In fact, we have 14 different common law definitions: one for each province and one for each of three territories, none of which are identical.

SUSAN CARTER

There is, at the moment, a significant amount of work being done in probably half the provinces on these issues. The whole objective of linking up what is happening at the federal and the provincial levels is, I think, a pretty important dimension. It is certainly something that we are going to be doing within the various sectors of the federal and provincial voluntary sectors and I think it will be very important to do that at the government level as well. I would not see it as bringing the provinces into this initiative, but of connecting the pieces that are underway on different fronts.

[Editor's Note: the provinces are being informed of developments in the Voluntary Sector Initiative but are not formally engaged in the process.]

GERDA KAEGI
Nonprofit and Voluntary Sector Management Programme
Ryerson University

My understanding of the Voluntary Sector Initiative is that the advocacy table is not funded. And yet my understanding from the discussions today is that there is 50/50 representation at the joint-table meetings — 50 percent federal civil servants and 50 percent from the nonprofit and voluntary sector. Also, and again I am looking at issues of representation, who do you see as representing the voluntary sector, executive directors or volunteers? My last comment is that it is my understanding that no seniors are sitting on those joint tables and no representatives from specific women's organizations in Canada. This is the thinking out in the public domain and I would like very much to hear that most of my concerns are incorrect.

SUSAN CARTER

The people on the joint tables are a mix of staff and volunteers, about a quarter of the people who sit on the tables are there in their capacity as volunteers. Nearly everyone is active as a volunteer in addition to being a staff member. There is a representative from a large seniors organization in Quebec and the president of that organization sits on the advocacy table. There are at least two representatives from women's organizations: DAWN, the Disabled Women's Network, and the president of the Féderation des femmes de Québec sits on the advocacy working group.

AL HATTON
National Voluntary Organisations

I think it is really important to keep in context what it is that is going on in the relationship with the federal government. We do not have to cast our minds back very far to characterize the relationship which we are now worrying about for some very good reasons and I appreciate Arthur's call for us not to be caught up too much in the rhetoric of partnership. We need to be cautious about our gains and to be very conscious of where we came from and who we really represent. We have to remember that this is part of a long process. Susan Carter talked about the voluntary sector being at the table with some of the same characters for a long time. There is a reason for that. It is because we are trying to build something very different and so, in fact, government people can come and go, voluntary sector can come and go, but we will not change our stripes all that much. We will continue to work on the things that we have been talking about for many years in this country.

When we were called special interest groups we were not special. In fact, by that label, we were more irrelevant than when we were simply voluntary organizations. It was a label intended to put us into a category that said we were like this which was, in fact, quite negative. It actually came from central agencies, not from frontline departments and people who knew the sector. We have to understand what their purposes are. Susan did point out the difference between government and the voluntary sector. We have very different ways of going about things and at times we have different purposes despite similar words. When I really got involved at the federal level in the late 1980s, the "third sector" was labour. The tripartide aspect of public policy was labour, government, and business.

The question of representation is a difficult one. We need a person with a disability on the committee. What are we going to do about the Aboriginal people? What are we going to do about rural Canadians? But, by and large, it was an individual who came to represent all that and I was one of the first people in some of those processes in the labour market side who said, "Wait a minute. Any one person, any hundred people can't represent the diversity and richness out there so this is unacceptable." By us saying this is unacceptable, means that we are no longer at the table. Five to ten years from now we may have conferences like this going on around the country, struggling with what is this, this other thing that we have misunderstood, we have overlooked, we have assumed does all these wonderful things for Canadians and you know what? This is good. Does it need to be sustained? Probably not. Can it be abused? Probably so. So in a sense, think about what this relationship represents. Comments like "This is all crap and it isn't going to work" are very shortsighted. Comments like "This is going to save the world" and suddenly the voluntary sector and everybody is wonderful and everybody is going to live happily ever after are not right either.

PADDY BOWEN
Volunteer Canada

I have a tiny technical point. Patrick, you talked about when someone gives $500 to the government, then in effect the society contributes a matching amount, that is only if that person gives that $500 to a political party. Otherwise, it is about 17 percent and as a citizen who donates a fair amount of money, I do not seem to get a big tax break from it.

DIXON SOOKRAJ
Okanagan University College

We have said very little about a specific component of the nonprofit sector, the organizations that contract with government to deliver public services. I wonder where the panel would classify many of these organizations given that they are heavily dependent on government for their funding, they deliver public services, and their traditional missions are compromised by the need to follow government policies, regulations and procedures. As Susan Fletcher said, they can be considered part of the whole process. There are two parts to the not-for-profit sector of the voluntary sector: the well-organized associations representing established parts of society, such as the Toronto Real Estate Board. There is an association of such organizations and as part of the Voluntary Sector Initiative process, they have been tracking this process and want to be more involved. The other part of the voluntary sector, which is the informal part, is less organized with entities that are not incorporated and many are not charities. They are involved but they are a little harder to reach.

PANEL TWO

DEMOCRACY, CIVIL SOCIETY AND THE STATE

MONICA PATTEN
President and Chief Executive Officer
Community Foundations of Canada

Working with the Federal Government: Community-Building and Civil Society

I will begin this paper with some remarks about both community-building and civil society, and then to try to link them to some ideas about how government is and can be an effective actor in the agenda of building community.

"Building community" is a hot topic these days, and I, like many others, am beginning to think that the phrase is overworked and perhaps somewhat unclear in meaning. As I speak about community-building in the context of this presentation, I am going to be speaking about geographically defined places where efforts are intentionally being made to strengthen and enhance the quality of life for people who live there. I think, though, that one could apply the characteristics I am about to mention to other forms of community as well — communities of interest or communities that claim a larger geographic boundary than may first be obvious.

If we can agree that strong and resilient communities are the goal of community-building, we are challenged collectively to find ways to support people in discovering and adapting to new structures, especially in changing family, workplace environments, and our multicultural society, and to do so in ways that do not completely abandon the past simply because it is "old" or because it is the past but in ways that connect the past to the present and to the future. We are challenged to encourage and support people to take responsibility for each other, for neighbours, kin and colleagues, and for themselves. We are challenged to make sure that those who are marginalized and isolated, for whatever reason, can participate in community life and that there are both formal and informal volunteer possibilities available for those who wish to become engaged. We are challenged to find ways to welcome newcomers, their histories, traditions and experiences, and to honour those who have deep roots in the community. We are challenged to encourage links and bonds within the community as well as beyond the community, using new forms of technology as well as building on existing relationships as well as new ones. And finally, we are challenged collectively to encourage and support new ideas and new forms of joint action to support community life, that is, we are challenged to invest in social capital because there is an appreciation and a knowledge that social capital produces trust and a willingness to work together, connections that benefit the community.

So community-building is about strengthening associational life — the collective life of the inhabitants of a community. Obviously, this is only one aspect of community-building. There is also maintaining a marketplace that provides employment, goods and services, economic opportunities. And it is about having formal democratic institutions in place that encourage justice and equality, that invite participation, and that are transparent and accountable. When we are discussing community-building, I am talking about all of these aspects.

Let me now turn to the words "civil society" (also a much used concept). I read that there are some 34,000 Web sites that make reference to civil society or have a significant part of their material devoted to the concept. There are lots of ways of defining and understanding it. I want to talk about civil society in connection with building community. When we discuss building strong, healthy, resilient, and vibrant communities, are we really saying that we are building a civil society? I am going to resist the temptation to go the definitional road here. Rather, I would like to say that I accept that civil society means individual and collective action working toward some common and public good and I think, unlike some others, that there is a role for various actors — government, the private sector, and the voluntary sector — in building civil society.

Let me try and describe a few reasons why I think the discussion about healthy, civil society is so important and why building this is also important. I then want to demonstrate the close link between civil society and community-building and then to explain some of the roles that government and the voluntary sector, in particular, can play in building civil society and building community. The western democratic context is the point of departure here, but I recognize that in, say, eastern or central Europe there might be different emphases and priorities when we are talking about building civil society.

First, a strong civil society is important because it encourages and allows for multiple sentries of opinion, deliberation, and public discussion and welcomes the voices of many. Democracy is surely strengthened with this kind of discourse. I stress that not for a moment am I thinking or speaking about "group think." It is precisely through variety of opinion and information that civil society and democracy are strengthened. So too, is community strengthened.

Second, social capital gets built when we have a strong civil society. Alexis De Toqueville saw that associational life was a school for democracy. It is within associational life that we learn habits of civility, we build trust and cooperative, interactive ways of behaving. Community-building is about precisely the same process. It is about working together to achieve commonly desired ends. It is here that I note that building associational life is not always formal. While some would argue that building civil society is always intentional and directed toward small "p" political outcomes (as may be the case in emerging democracies), others would argue that being part of a fitness group at the local community centre is also about building civil society or building associational or community life.

Third, civil society is generally the place and the space where charity occurs, that is, where citizens can share their resources of time and money to benefit their community, over and above what they are required to do as duties of formal citizenship such as paying taxes. Again, this is an important feature of community-building. The question then of building community and building civil society and how similar they are, in my view, can be answered by saying that in this context, they are indeed quite similar.

Who then contributes what to the building of community and civil society? I have already stated my own belief that there is room, indeed perhaps must be room, for multiple players. Each has an independent role as well as interdependent roles. I would like to focus on some ideas about those roles.

Let me begin with government. Government maintains and promotes the formal institutions of democracy. Within that role, it (and I am speaking about government in the singular but I recognize that various levels of government have the same responsibilities) develops and implements just systems so that all citizens can have access to certain levels of security in areas of income, safety, learning opportunities, or health care. Another role is to ensure that the rights of citizens are known and upheld and that marginalized and silent voices can be part of the public discourse. Still another is to create frameworks and structures that encourage participation (through an income tax structure, for example) and that bring information and knowledge about how government works in order to strengthen democracy. One example in Canada, obviously, would be the Community Access Points. There is a legitimate expectation that government will both anticipate and respond to changing environments and, of course, display the highest levels of accountability and transparency in all that they do.

Economic institutions and the private sector are also significant players in building community. Their role in contributing to prosperity is evident. Their role as good corporate citizens — working with others to achieve social good and benefit at the same time as meeting their own ends — is equally important but less well understood and evident. I have just returned from a trip to Brazil to a conference that focused on corporate philanthropy and community philanthropy which is just beginning to emerge in that country. Their corporate leaders spoke about their commitment with a passion that I have not heard in this country. We are deeply challenged to lift and raise those voices in Canada in the way that they are being heard in other parts of the world.

The role of the voluntary sector can also be enunciated and is in many documents and in other places: developing and delivering services and programs; inspiring and mobilizing action on the part of individuals and groups of citizens; challenging the status quo and informing citizens on issues, priorities and trends; raising funds; holding up a vision; contributing to policy; and much much more. The litany is familiar.

The question then becomes: How do all of these players work together? For our purposes here, how do government and the voluntary sector work together to build community, and to strengthen civil society? First, more discussion of respective, broad goals, and broad roles is necessary. It is probably an overstatement to say that government and voluntary sector always share the same broad goals. The reality is that sometimes we do not and we probably should not in order to avoid being co-opted. But we have, in fact, made some assumptions about that and we couched them in broad and somewhat vague terms: for example, we say that we are working for the betterment of Canadian society. We share that in common. We need to understand a little bit more about what that means. We have tended to mask the distinctions while doing little to elaborate on the similarities. The voluntary sector, in particular, needs to better understand and articulate its broad role and value in building community, in building civil society, recognizing that it is only one of several players, both formal and informal.

A second step would be to articulate the nature of relationships in a time when governance is changing. "Citizen-focused services," "citizen engagement," "partnerships," are all buzzwords in government today as well as the voluntary sector though I am not always sure that we attach the same meaning to those words. We both talk about accountability, about transparency and accessibility. We first need to sort out some broad goals and roles and what we each bring to the parade; and then we need to consider the language and the words that adequately reflect our own governance approaches. We need to sort out how we are going to behave together: Are we interested in joint planning, in assignment of specific roles in program or service delivery, in the implementation of common practices and measures of outcome, in the development of common messages? How will our behaviours and actions get us closer to reaching our separate and mutual goals?

If we can be clear about these broad goals and roles in community-building, what we each have to offer that is faithful to our values and our principles, the way we use language to reflect our approaches and the specifics of how we will behave together, we will be able to share successfully in community-building and building civil society. But to get to that place requires trust, time, relationship-building, respect, willingness to take risks, willingness to compromise, and appreciation for the constraints and the realities that we are all facing in our respective sectors. Rather than assuming that we can accomplish all of this at once, I suggest that we, in the words of one of Canada's largest banks, "build this one customer at a time." We need to identify some common community-building that is already underway or some new work that is about to begin and examine it, revise it as it goes along, and develop it as appropriate. We need to consider the lessons learned and broadly disseminate those experiences — something we do very poorly in both sectors.

There is common ground for building community, but we have many miles to travel together if we are going to realize the full benefit of our relationship and be truly able to do that together. We both need to keep in mind that the relationship is not the end in itself. The working together is not the end in itself. Stronger communities and a healthy civil society are the goals.

RAINER KNOPFF
Professor of Political Science
University of Calgary

Civil Society vs. Democracy

This essay argues that "civil society," which is correctly presented as an essential foundation for liberal democracy, has become the basis of an anti-democratic rhetoric. The term is being used to shift the aura of democratic legitimacy from more representative to less representative institutions.

Civil society is the realm of groups and associations that exist between the individual and the state. A healthy civil society, it is argued, generates the "social capital" — the social trust — required by both representative institutions and a market economy.[1] In Robert Putnam's famous formulation, a society is better off if people bowl in organized leagues than if they go "bowling alone."[2] There are, of course, downsides to the associative activity of civil society. Criminal organizations are also a part of civil society, and one may well wonder whether it isn't better for criminals to go it alone than in Mafia-like leagues. Still, on the whole, Putnam is right. A vigorous civil society is on balance a good thing. At any rate, it has come to be seen as *such* a good thing that both sides of the political spectrum enthusiastically embrace it as the cure for what ails us. But, as one would expect, the left and the right differ markedly on how civil society should cure us and, as usual, the difference turns in good measure on the issue of state involvement.[3]

The issue of service delivery provides an example. In an era of at least partial state retrenchment, both sides see civil society as an alternative way to

The author wishes to thank the Donner Canadian Foundation for its financial support.

[1]See Robert Putnam, *Making Democracy Work: Civic Traditions in Modern Italy* (Princeton, NJ: Princeton University Press, 1993); and Francis Fukuyama, *Trust: The Social Virtues and the Creation of Prosperity* (London: Penguin, 1995).

[2]Robert Putnam, *Bowling Alone: The Collapse and Revival of American Community* (New York: Simon & Schuster, 2000).

[3]See William A. Galston, "Civil Society and the 'Art of Association,'" *Journal of Democracy* 11,1 (2000): 64. D.W. Miller, "Perhaps We Bowl Alone, but Does it Really Matter," *Chronicle of Higher Education*, 16 July 1999.

deliver social services. When the right speaks of "alternative service delivery" by civil society groups, it tends to have in mind service delivery that is independent of the state. For much of the right, the central problem with the modern welfare state is that it has taken over too many services that used to be provided by civil society, and has weakened civil society in the process. In speaking of alternative service delivery, in other words, the right sees its favoured civil-society organizations as true alternatives to the state, alternatives that work best when the state leaves them room and leaves them alone.

The left, by contrast, seeks more active "partnerships" between the state and civil society groups. The left's disagreement with the right on this issue was well expressed by Finance Minister Paul Martin during the Human Resources Develoment Canada funding scandal. "The Reform Party," said Martin, "does not believe that there is a role for government in working with Kinsmen clubs, Richelieu clubs, Optimist clubs, Lions clubs, Rotary clubs." In contrast, said Martin, Liberals "believe that there is a responsibility of the federal government to work with communities across the country and we are going to continue to do so."[4] When he said, "work with," Martin meant providing civil society groups with tangible resources, especially money.

Partnerships between government and civil society groups exist not just to deliver services, of course, but to further political agendas. Just think of the partnership of the Trudeau government and a variety of interest groups against the "gang of eight" provinces during the Charter-making process.[5]

The partnership phenomenon is deeply ironic. On the one hand, its proponents present it as a democratic advance. On the other hand, it has generally involved the weakening of representative institutions in favour of less representative ones. It is part of what an American commentator calls the rise of the "new executive state."[6]

Consider the increasingly prominent partnership between the United Nations and non-governmental organizations (NGOs). International NGOs are

---

[4]Paul Wells, "Poof! Out Pops the Amazing Prestoni and Liberals Explode," *National Post*, 24 February 2000.

[5]See Rainer Knopff and F.L. Morton, "Nation-Building and the Canadian Charter of Rights and Freedoms," in *Constitutionalism, Citizenship and Society in Canada*, ed. Alan Cairns and Cynthia Williams (Toronto: University of Toronto Press, 1985).

[6]Christopher C. DeMuth, "After the Ascent: Politics and Government in the Super-Affluent Society," Francis Boyer Lecture, Washington, DC: American Enterprise Institute for Public Policy Research, 15 February 2000. At <http://www.aei.org/boyer/demuth.htm>.

now often referred to as "global civil society,"[7] and this concept is sometimes used to challenge national sovereignty and domestic democracy in the name of so-called global democracy. From the increasingly archaic nation-state, power flows both down, to civil society and multicultural groups, and up, to world institutions. Since there is no global electorate, international civil society is presented as the basis of democratic legitimacy for world institutions. For example, UN Secretary-General Kofi Annan has referred to "the NGO revolution" as "the new global people-power,"[8] which "information technology has empowered to be the true guardian of democracy and good governance everywhere."[9] The fact that no elections are involved in the new global democracy is irrelevant, since morally pure NGOs are more in tune with the people's true needs and desires than are actual governments, who are often "elected" on the basis of fraud, manipulation, and the false consciousness of voters — if, indeed, they are elected at all

Or consider the equally prominent domestic partnership between civil society and the courts. Charles Epp has published a very fine book arguing that the "rights revolution" — which he quite clearly associates with the growth of judicial power — is caused not primarily by documents or judges but by interest groups effectively mobilizing legal resources in the courts.[10] A rights revolution, Epp insists, depends mainly on what he calls a "support structure for legal mobilization." Epp's marshalling of comparative evidence in support of this proposition is impressive and persuasive. What is contentious is Epp's

---

[7]See the speech given to the Canadian Parliament by Vaclav Havel, president of the Czech Republic, on 29 April 1999. See also Ann Marie Clark, Elisabeth J. Friedman and Kathryn Hochstetler, "The Sovereign Limits of Global Civil Society: A Comparison of NGO Participation in UN World Conferences on the Environment, Human Rights, and Women," *World Politics* 51,1(1998). The term "international civil society" is also used by Dianne Otto, "Nongovernmental Organizations in the United Nations System: The Emerging Role of International Civil Society," *Human Rights Quarterly* 18,1 (1996). Another synonym is "world civil society": Gordon A. Christenson, "World Civil Society and the International Rule of Law," *Human Rights Quarterly* 19:4 (1997).

[8]Quoted in "The Uncivil Society," *National Post*, 13 December 1999.

[9]Quoted in Richard John Neuhaus, "Forget the Bilderbergers," *First Things* February 2000, p. 79.

[10]Charles R. Epp, *The Rights Revolution: Lawyers, Activists, and Supreme Courts in Comparative Perspective* (Chicago: University of Chicago Press, 1998).

claim that a support structure for legal mobilization not only causes a rights revolution but also renders it democratic: "If the rights revolution developed out of the growth of a broad support structure in *civil society* ... then the rights revolution was not undemocratic or anti-democratic."[11]

Notice the parallel with the global democracy argument. Just as global civil society provides a democratic justification for UN power, so domestic civil society provides a democratic justification for growing judicial power. In both cases, the result is to justify increased power for less representative institutions (the UN, courts) at the expense of more representative ones (legislatures). The less representative institutions acquire democratic legitimacy by virtue of a direct link with the people, organized in civil society organizations.

This argument involves two interrelated and equally suspect rhetorical moves:

1. Interest groups are re-labelled as civil-society groups or the "third sector." The claim that *interest* groups should bypass representative legislatures is rhetorically more difficult to sustain than that "civil society" groups should do so.

2. The democratic credentials of legislatures are called into question. There are two parts to this argument:

    (a) *Legislatures are not terribly democratic either.* There is actually considerable truth to this claim,[12] though, of course, it begs the question why unelected judges or NGOs should be considered *more* democratic. To address this question we must go to the second point.

    (b) *Legislatures are less morally attractive than courts or NGOs.* One reason is that legislatures respond to narrow *interests*, which are guided by unreflecting *passions*, while courts and NGOs respond to (or reflect*) civil society*; this, of course, returns us to the first rhetorical move.

Not surprisingly, these rhetorical moves do not attract general agreement. To the claims of global democracy, for example, Richard Neuhaus replies: "Globaloney."[13] In practice, he argues, global democracy means making global

---

[11]Ibid., p. 5. Emphasis added.

[12]See, e.g., Donald Savoie, *Governing from the Centre: The Concentration of Power in Canadian Politics* (Toronto: University of Toronto Press, 1999).

[13]Neuhaus, "Forget the Bilderbergers," p. 77.

government "accountable to the NGOs, which in turn, are accountable to no-body but the philanthropies that fund them and their own, typically very small, memberships."[14] Neuhaus concludes that

> "Global Governance and Democracy within the Global State" means that small groups are able to make rules affecting the domestic affairs of countries that it would have been difficult or impossible to achieve democratically in those countries. Global Democracy is, in fact, an end run around democracy.[15]

In Lorne Gunter's pithy formulation, the objective is to give "the UN and its NGO friends ... as much control over domestic policies and laws as the elected government of a country."[16] This is a form of "globalization" that appeals to some of its most vociferous critics.

Neuhaus also draws the connection between "the UN-NGO nexus" on the international stage and judicial policy-making on the domestic stage. "Whether through the UN or through judicial lawmaking," he says, "the result is the usurpation of democratic politics."[17] From this perspective, Epp's support structure for legal mobilization looks more like a Court Party.[18]

Ironically, the rhetorical use of civil society to "democratize" such unelected bodies as the UN and the judiciary furthers the already pronounced strengthening of the political executive at the expense of the legislature. The executive often allies itself with civil society constituencies to achieve international agreements or court decisions that can be used to justify ramming controversial policies through the legislature, arguing that the constitution[19] or our international commitments[20] leave us no choice. Indeed, the courts sometimes read

---

[14]Ibid., p. 78.

[15]Ibid., p. 79.

[16]Lorne Gunter, "A Mecca for the Left," *National Post*, 24 September 1999.

[17]Neuhaus, "Forget the Bilderbergers," p. 79.

[18]See F.L. Morton and Rainer Knopff, *The Charter Revolution and the Court Party* (Peterborough: Broadview Press, 2000).

[19]For example, this is how the federal government justified the extension of common-law status to same sex couples in *An Act to Modernize the Statutes of Canada in Relation to Benefits and Obligations* (Bill C-23, 2000). See also, Morton and Knopff, *The Charter Revolution and the Court Party*, pp. 117-20.

[20]Lorne Gunter, "Playing with the World's Agenda," *National Post*, 30 August 1999.

international developments into the constitution,[21] thereby completing a tight circle that leaves out representative legislatures. Rhetorical move 2(a) above uses the decline of legislatures to justify the search for greater "democracy" in civil society. The result is a self-fulfilling prophecy, in which an alliance of courts, international institutions, and the domestic executive further marginalizes legislatures. A truly vicious circle.

In 1977 Neuhaus and Peter Berger wrote *To Empower People*, an influential manifesto about "mediating institutions" that helped launch the contemporary interest in civil society.[22] Ironically, as Neuhaus points out, the original idea, which was to limit government and make it more accountable, is now being used to expand the scope of the state's most unaccountable institutions.[23]

AL HATTON
Executive Director
National Voluntary Organisations

The Importance of Building Civil Society

Civil society, does, at its best, build democracy. It brings people out, in order to have them work with other people, learn skills, work in communities, give to their neighbours, look at what is going on in the community or what is going on in the larger community if it is not geographic and, in fact, build partnerships, challenge people in a way that we often do not find at work and we often do not find in government. This exercise does not just stop at building democracy, but is also about creating a new form of governance. When we talked about governance before, a lot of people thought we meant government. Now it is not that simple. It is about governance, but we do not have the mechanisms nor the processes and we do not have the leaders who understand that

---

[21]See, for example, *United States v. Burns* 2001 SCC 7, regarding extradition without assurances that capital punishment will not be applied.

[22]Peter L. Berger and Richard John Neuhaus, *To Empower People*, ed. Michael Novak, 12th anniversary edition. (Washington, DC: AEI Press, 1996).

[23]Neuhaus, "Forget the Bilderbergers," p. 78.

something new is happening. The question becomes how can we institutional- ize new forms of governing in a way that we do not destroy that creativity and thus return to the past?

More and more groups and more and more people are talking about co- governance. Civil society is not just about government. The solution, at least in the developed world, is not just to try and dust off representative democracy and make it work. So what is the alternative? The alternative is to find a brand new way for the voluntary sector and government to work together. Partner- ship will not work because they need to involve equals and this is not an asso- ciation of equals. Fundamentally it is about getting citizens involved, I think, having organizations take part in the process of governance. The roles will be very different for citizens, organizations, and government. One does not re- place the other. But if you start to engage citizens, then organizations become engaged, governments become engaged, along with the private sector and la- bour, and then something magical and new happens.

The second thing that civil society does is to encourage people to partici- pate — alone or with other people. Even if you are bowling alone, there is somebody else in the next lane. And with bowlers as awkward as I am the ball probably goes into the other lane anyway. This is about getting people involved with others. It is about inspiring people to become re-engaged in their commu- nity, wanting to make a contribution, becoming involved. It is very hard to do given the stress people face, but it is still at the core, the central thing that the voluntary sector does.

Third, civil society builds social cohesion, social capital, and resilient com- munities when it works. When it does not work, it quickly becomes obvious, but at its best it brings people together, it has them doing things cooperatively, it gets them solving problems and learning how to work with their neighbours.

And the last area is something that we have tended to overlook. We debate universal programs, who can and cannot afford them and the failure of the welfare state, but we overlook the magic of the welfare state and the fantastic things it does do. In part, the welfare state is about finding a way to deal with those who are marginalized, finding a way to involve the socially excluded. We are caught up in a new mantra, the Internet, because it can be an effective tool for reaching people. The fundamental way in which we reach people is as important today as it was 20 years ago without the technology. We have to find new and better ways to reach others. We need to find ways to engage citizens, to link people up and down in bureaucracies, and within systems so they can begin to talk to each other.

Those are just four areas of definitional challenge. I do not want to define civil society, but I think it is important that we have a bit of a sense of this concept from a few points of view. Is the Ku Klux Klan part of civil society? It is membership-based. It is non-governmental. It would argue it has, when people come to them, a democratic process. They elect a leader and thus they could argue "we're part of civil society." My sense is, over time, they will exclude themselves when they realize that we are trying to support communities, to live by the UN convention, and to *include* people in society. We should not spend a lot of time worrying about this. People self-select their way in and people of like minds start building and rebuilding communities and societies so that more people will have the benefits of living in a community. In a sense you might say the Ku Klux Klan under that definition might be the *uncivil* part of civil society. Our view has been to try to be inclusive, not exclusive. In fact, our experiences show that most people can deal with those who are different.

The second perspective on civil society is that government and business are a definite part of the whole movement. We need to find ways for all of our structures and systems to work together. Some people employed by corporations and government already give of their time and are part of civil society. But we have got to find better ways of including people to build on their differences and strengths.

Why is this important for Canada now? I think we are at a particular juncture. The voluntary sector has undergone massive cuts. We know that. We have faced some challenges to our legitimacy — not as individual organizations but as a collective. There is no question, we have been buffeted and pressed to be more and more like the corporate sector. Parts of that are really, really good. Some is really, really scary. We have to figure out which is which in order to be true to our missions and our purposes as a particular kind of organization. There is still the classic debate about whether, in fact, we can afford the programs that help those who are excluded. Concurrently, there has been a massive rise in the reach and influence of the private sector. In a sense we have mixed up the idea of business being able to create a healthy economy with the notion of business being able to create a healthy society. Obviously, it is not believable that business can do the latter. While these changes in the voluntary and business sectors have taken place, government has been drawing back. It is not just about fiinancial cuts. Government has been drawing back, questioning its purpose, questioning what it has been doing, and we have seen the things around downsizing: devolution, growth of regionalism, focus on the economy, and on and on.

That is what we have been through. We are now moving into a different era. These trends are part of a global movement: a global revolution. Lester Salamon at Johns Hopkins University is doing some fascinating research on global associations and their evolution. He is discovering that across the globe, civil society is actually growing faster in many countries than the private sector is. In the 22 countries measured, including developing countries, eastern bloc countries, and Organisation of Economic Co-operation and Development (OECD) countries, the civil society sector would amount to the world's eighth largest economy. It has more employees than the largest private firms in every one of those countries. It out-distances numerous industries like utilities, paper, and chemicals. That figure excludes the volunteer sector which is roughly an additional 28 percent in terms of output across those countries.

Civil society is thriving across the globe as well as here at home. I was struck by the profound outpouring of emotion when the former prime minister, Pierre Elliott Trudeau, died in September 2000. It was not partisan or about the Liberal Party, although some people in the Liberal Party might wish that it was. His death touched a chord in many Canadians. A large number of young people and immigrants came out and spoke about the kind of country they wanted, not the kind of province they wanted, not the kind of neighbourhood they wanted, the kind of country they wanted. There is something there to pay attention to.

Why is it important to involve the voluntary sector in governance now? We have government budgetary surpluses at the federal level and in almost every province. Soon all the provinces will be in that position. Most citizens, despite what polls say, understand that even in a surplus position, government cannot do everything alone and the private sector is not going to undertake the huge problems of building healthier societies. The voluntary sector becomes more necessary than ever. At the national level, we are talking in terms of building a new relationship with both the private sector and the other major actors in society. We also need to strengthen this sector domestically and globally in order to be a major player in building healthier societies. A recent study that the Canadian Centre for Philanthropy carried out with resources from the Muttart Foundation demonstrates that generally Canadians have high trust levels for voluntary organizations and their ability to undertake this task.

In addition to the topics addressed here, there is a brand new way for the voluntary sector in Canada to work. When we went through the program review a number of individuals asked, "What are we going to do differently? How are we going to become strategic? How are we going to become proactive? How are we going to get ahead of this wave toward the private sector sweeping across the globe that isn't recognizing our value?" As an outcome, a number of national organizations created the umbrella agency known as the voluntary sector roundtable (VSR). We have done the same thing with children's organizations, with health charities, and with youth groups. We are bringing a number of these groups together to talk strategically about what we can do on behalf of our constituents to improve our involvement in public policy and the way in which we operate and strategize. We have already put a lot of energy into this.

The same period has witnessed the growth of provincial networks. Increasingly, what the voluntary sector roundtable has been doing at the federal level is being replicated — but in a different way, with different issues, by different organizations in many of the provinces. That activity will be one of the vehicles for applying pressure on the provinces to come to the table with the federal government to begin to have more effective social policies. Frankly, the impetus for provincial involvement in the Voluntary Sector Initiative needs to come from the provinces and not from the federal government. It if comes from the top down it is not going to work. Another source of pressure on the provinces to become more involved comes from the International Year of Volunteers 2001 (IYV). IYV will be a great opportunity to profile both the contribution of volunteers and the voluntary sector. Already, both levels of government are beginning to work together more cooperatively, for example, the social union framework agreement. However, there needs to be more cooperation on social policy and the voluntary sector needs to become much more involved.

Government and voluntary organizations also have to engage the business sector in this task. The Canadian Centre for Philanthropy is putting an important effort forward with the *Imagine* campaign, and the Conference Board and their campaign on corporate social responsibility. They are emphasizing the need to be "working together now." This effort to engage the corporate sector in giving and participating is a very important development.

What are some of the challenges? While we have already been thinking like a sector we have to act more like a sector. The means of engaging citizens remains a major challenge. We do not have the resources or the capacity to do it properly. We have to find better ways, especially with those who are excluded or marginalized. A companion issue — and this is a big issue in the sector — is that organizations do not automatically represent citizens. They do not automatically speak for groups of citizens outside their own membership and their own constituency. This is a problem. If we say that we are building a civil society, then what is our relationship to elected representatives and to citizens? How can we be more accountable? This is important since we are not accountable in some of the areas we have been discussing. How do we create the new instruments to improve accountability?

You are going to hear in other papers about *capacity*. We need to be involved in more research in order to ensure that our story is told.

SELECTED COMMENTS FROM THE DISCUSSION

SID FRANKEL

Voluntary Sector Council in Manitoba

One of the observations I would make is that both in the public discourse and in the academic discourse, the role of the sector seems to be defined almost exclusively in terms of the failure of other sectors rather than in terms of the strength of the voluntary sector. We have original theories of failure of markets and the necessity for a voluntary sector or failure of private philanthropy. More laterally we have theories from the left and right to explain the failure of the welfare state and now even the failure of democratic institutions and perhaps the failure of informal community. It strikes me that the voluntary sector always seems to be defined in residual terms because something else that is "more legitimate" really should be there but has failed.

The second observation I would make is that, of course, these versions of failure of other sectors are contested versions or they contest each other. Not only is the voluntary sector defined in terms of failure of "more legitimate" sectors but these versions of failure argue with each other and it seems to me that that kind of discourse makes it very hard to sort this out.

RAINER KNOPFF

It is true that a lot of the thinking here has to do with failure of some sectors and bringing the voluntary sector in is a cure or bringing civil society in is a cure. The one that I was concerned with, of course, is the failure of the democratic sector (the legislature, the sector of representative government) that is usually attributed to, especially in the Canadian case, the tremendous growth of executive domination. It is interesting that statements are being made such as, "Let's not solve that by tinkering with the structure of representative government. Let's just give up on that and do it in a new way by turning to the voluntary sector." The voluntary sector will now partner with that same executive-dominated government. I am going to suggest that the result of that will be to further exacerbate the executive domination of our government. It may be in ways that will help the voluntary sector and that may not: surpluses or excess taxation. If it is excess taxation, rather than surpluses, why does the voluntary sector have to partner with the executive branch of government in deciding how to spend the extra money they have taken out of our pockets?

Let me now make the most contentious suggestion: cut taxes, get rid of all those rules that Patrick Monahan was talking about, eliminate any more tax credits and tax deductions, and so on. Cut taxes and let people decide where they want to put their money, which may even include the voluntary sector.

AL HATTON

It is maybe not even that simple: maybe the voluntary sector has also failed because we have not been at the table, have not stepped forward with what it is we do in a way that people can really understand and believe in a collective way, so I would rather not talk about the failure of all the systems. We have an opportunity to do things a bit differently and that is what this is about. We do not have pat answers. We are experimenting and it is risky. We are giving something up in the hope that we can be in a better place. So this is also about independence. It is not just about sidling up with the authorities and being part of a new series of decisions in a balanced approach. Every government is doing the same thing. They are all trying to deal with their debt, deficits and investments, so surplus may be the wrong word. There will be new money for investments and there will be a fight about who gets the benefits. In the past, we were not even at the table. We were not considered. Some were as individuals, but we were not collectively. So rather than apportioning blame, the challenge is to start thinking differently about how we get from here to a better place, how we involve more people, serve more people in better ways and more efficiently than we did in the past. This is the real challenge.

Another issue came up during Rainer Knopff's comments. We have to be careful when people disagree with us and we say, "Oh there they go. That's the same old thing. It's a way to undermine us." I think he asked some very profound questions and frankly we do not have the answers to a lot of those questions. We are struggling. How do we involve people? The democratic process has its flaws. Many in the community would argue that in practice democracy does not work. For example, if a citizen were to try and influence the US election, except by a vote, that citizen would need to be rich, obscenely rich. There is no place, in fact, for community organizations and for processes to get individuals involved in a way that they can exercise influence over the matters they are concerned about when they can only vote for two parties and there is hardly a difference between them. If that is what democracy has become, we have a major problem. I would also suggest that some of the so-called representatives of the community that we call a global civil society, are in fact, simply a countermeasure against the corporate structure. They are not saying they speak for citizens in every country of the world on every issue of concern to citizens. They are simply saying that there is another power structure above national governments and that is the threat to the world, to the environment, to human development, to people in poor countries, and this is where the fight begins. There are a number of important questions that need to be addressed. The current process may fall short of the mark in answering all these considerations, but maybe it is better than what we have. We just need to ask ourselves how we can make it better.

PADDY BOWEN
Volunteer Canada

Some of your remarks, Rainer, made me think about something that is completely unrelated to these larger issues that we are talking about, but before I get to that point, you used a quote. "We used to refer to them as interest groups." I have worked in the sector for 20 years and I have never worked for something I called an "interest group."

You talked about a romantic view of when civil society used to do it all. We did not call it civil society in those days. What it was, depending on how far back you go, was the church and faith communities who bore the responsibility for serving Canadians. There is currently a fascinating, and for me very dismaying, story unfolding in the voluntary sector in Canada that implicates government, the courts and the church as we see what may be the elimination of the Anglican Church of Canada and the United Church of Canada, as well as the severe beating taken by the Roman Catholic Church of Canada for their role in the residential schools. I attended a lecture on this recently and learned that it is the Government of Canada that is naming the churches as the third party in the cases, not the plaintiffs. The government, in lieu of taking perhaps a legislative or social policy approach to dealing with this issue and bearing responsibility, is involving the churches who are implicated through the actions of the people who worked for the churches. Those individuals are being held accountable in the criminal courts, but through the instrument of the courts, the government is divesting its responsibility and the upshot of it is that the only money going anywhere is going to lawyers. The churches have said quite clearly, "We are going to spend all our money on legal fees and will have no ability to redress the victims." Thus, the victims are being "hung out to dry" and we are going to see the end of the formal, certainly Protestant, mainline churches in Canada. The Catholic Church will be severely dented. This has further implications for the whole of the sector.

RAINER KNOPFF

This issue is serious. I do not know how much of the money is going to the lawyers, but certainly I expect that a fair amount of it is. A comparison can be made with the "tainted blood scandal." The government made a social policy decision to negotiate a compensation package and the lawyers are blamed for that because they received a substantial amount of that money. On the other hand, the lawyers negotiated the package. I guess the government must be saying to itself, in the residential schools case, is that they are prepared to let that happen.

Under our system of law, victims of this type of abuse are entitled to compensation, even though giving people money does not actually compensate them for what they have suffered. However, it is the only way that we deal with it and to deny those people would be unfair. The only other opportunity there would be is for taxpayers, through the government and the legislature, to step up and contribute. Presumably, there has been a decision made that there is no political support for this. That is a judgement that the government is obviously going to have to make when the consequences mentioned ultimately come to pass.

PETER WILSON
Ontario Public Health Association

There was a reference to the capacity of the voluntary sector to strengthen democracy. I would suggest that it probably strengthens any political system in which it operates. It could strengthen autocracy. It strengthened communist countries. I think, though, that in a broad sense we are sceptical of our relationship with government and I think that the efforts the voluntary sector roundtable is doing to engage in this is in itself saying, "Well, if the government wants to choose to be more secretive, at the very least we are not." What is our relationship? If we are throwing brick bats at the government, we should ask ourselves this. If our organizations are not democratic, if we are more autocracies than democratic organizations in the way that we elect our boards of directors and the way we engage our members, what are we telling them about democracy? How much are we "walking the walk" in relationship to the democratic process which, in fact, exacerbates the scepticism that people have about the democratic process in which we need to work?

AL HATTON

Well, the good thing about having such a diverse sector is you see the best and the worst. Organizations in the sector that really have as a core purpose to engage their constituents, tend to have more open processes, they leave decision-making to groups of people in local communities working on issues. The opposite is also true. There are organizations that are very corporate and centralized and structured so that the head office in Ottawa or Toronto is responsible for all the assets along with everything else. There are also others that are completely decentralized. There is no simple answer.

The best thing the Panel on Accountability and Governance in the Voluntary Sector chaired by Ed Broadbent did was send a mini-shock-wave across the sector about governance. When we first began thinking about the issue of accountability, everybody thought it was all about the bottom line and whether we were doing the right thing with the money. Then, organizations really began to reflect on their governance structures. Who is involved in making decisions? Whom do we really speak for? Who is making decisions: the staff or the board? What is a good governance model for a voluntary organization? Many were using the Carver model from the United States but now there are important doubts about that model. Some people currently involved in agencies are feeling that there should not be such a separation between volunteers and staff. Policy and operations cannot be separated that easily. When millions of dollars are involved, everyone is accountable. These are important questions.

RAINER KNOPFF

I would agree entirely that a healthy civil society sector is one of the mainstays, in Putnam's terms, "that makes democracy work." There is no question about that largely for the reasons that Toqueville originally sketched out. It is the sort of nursery school of interrelationships, trust, learning how to deal with others and with complex organizations and so on. All of which is essential. I do not agree that it supports all societies equally. I think the experience in the communist regime says that the two are incompatible and they destroy civil society. Part of the emergence of the whole notion of civil society came from the fact that after some of the communist regimes fell it was so hard to regenerate civic trust. There is some discussion of this in the literature. Francis Fukuyama, for example, talks about different kinds of civil society organizations in terms of how vertical they are and how horizontal they are. The latter, in his view, serve those Toquevillian functions much more effectively.

MICHAEL O'NEILL
Justice Canada

My question really links both panels. We are in a situation now because of cutbacks and other circumstances that were identified by Al Hatton and others, a situation where many programs or issues are being pushed down to the community level. In Justice Canada, we talk about involving communities in areas such as restorative justice or corrections programs, etc. We are moving things to the community level that should engage the voluntary sector: the John Howard Societies, the Elizabeth Fry Societies, and a number of other organizations.

However, at the same time as these issues are evolving to the community level, polls and surveys show that citizens "bowl alone," that they are no longer members of these organizations, that they want to have a direct say in government decision-making and they want to do this beyond their votes. We are now, in government circles anyway, using the buzzword, "citizen engagement." We are going over the heads of community organizations right to citizens themselves and asking them what they want, to identify the problems, and to help us identify the solutions. In a circumstance where we talk directly to citizens, what does this mean for the voluntary sector? Does it make the sector irrelevant or does it have to change its operating procedures in relationship to both citizens and government?

Where does government fit in relation to this? Does it continue to engage the voluntary sector and treat it as a partner or does it go directly to the citizen?

AL HATTON

One of the good things about having three people from the voluntary sector is that you often end up with three different opinions. Here, there is only one. It is a question of credibility and trust. I am not really worried about the voluntary sector becoming irrelevant because if it is becoming irrelevant then it is not involved with citizens at the local level. Government has to be very careful, I think, about going directly to the public. That experience has not been all that great for government because they end up responding to competing agendas. In a sense, we can play the role of being helpful by having better connections with the public. If you just want to hear what people think about an issue, it is easy enough to use polls. They will tell you this is what people think, 19 out of 20 times, but it is never that simple. To involve people is often very different.

We do not have the magic answer but if we cannot do it, it will be a lot harder for government. We have to find a way to do it together. Part of the challenge is how to use our collective resources to accomplish this.

MARILYN HAY
Human Resources Development Canada

In terms of just cutting taxes and seeing what happens, one model is the American system. It is fairly close and it has not addressed homelessness, the poor or undernourished children in the United States. They do have lower taxes, but I am not sure that is the complete answer. In a sense, it is too complex for any of us as a single piece — whether private sector, individual citizen, third sector, civil society or government — to solve any one problem. It is not enough to just be a benevolent government like we tried to be in the rich 1960s and 1970s. While we meant well, we created even more problems of dependency and perpetuated problems because people did not take part in their own solutions.

The question: "What kind of country do we want?" really strikes a chord. It is, in part, what this is about: how we generate the maximum number of individuals creating a place where everyone has access and the chance to contribute. For example, the most vulnerable children under age three get proper nutrition, security, and some intellectual stimulation to achieve their full potential without being dependent on social welfare. We can predict reasonably well before kids are born, just by their parents' address, whether or not they will end up in jail. The third sector is a way to engage citizens. It allows people who care and who will help to make a difference, who have the energy and personal commitment to get involved.

There is a difference between being responsible and being accountable. Accountability in my mind is linked to how we expend public funds. There is a need for accountability there, specifically when we engage third sector groups to deliver programs on our behalf, but there may not be a need to be accountable broadly to all citizens on the part of everybody in civil society. That is the job of the elected representatives.

One of the things I struggle with is the role of the media in all of this because that is part of how we define our national agenda and how we engage discussion, debate, and dialogue in Canada. I wonder how we might do a better job of drawing the media into these issues so they can in turn draw more Canadians into this kind of necessary discussion.

LLANA JAMES
Hamilton AIDS Network

What has not been presented in these two panels is location. There is a discussion about people and the third sector and voluntary organizations, but it has not been located in the context from which it has arisen. The discussion about the churches and the dioceses becoming bankrupt, along with the issue of tainted blood, speaks to the roots of the sector. The root is the missionary complex which means that voluntary organizations come from the ideal of getting into other people's business all over the world and messing with all kinds of people's issues in such a manner that they thought they could actually solve their problems. The voluntary sector, along with the elusive democratic society, is based within that milieux. I was hoping that the panel would add a different dimension but we keep talking about taxes, that is, people who have money. Obviously, the people here do not fulfill most of the requirements to be poor, to be the undernourished and those constituencies are not actually present.

Perhaps at the second gathering, we should look at context and reality and perhaps reduce the banter. There is real community participation at stake. Perhaps in a working group process, we could try to alleviate our problems and be more inclusive.

MICHAEL ORSINI
School of Public Administration
Carleton University

I am disturbed by this suggestion that somehow we need to return to the language of interest groups. I wonder perhaps where you would locate the contributions made by social movements such as the feminist movement or the environmental movement? Certainly, this is not a narrowly defined interest and I think that language generates more heat than light.

RAINER KNOPFF

When I said we used to talk about interest groups, I was referring to we: political scientists, social scientists. I also work for voluntary organizations and do not use the term there, but as an analyst I would maintain that there are very few saints in the world by definition, which is why when we find them we use them as models. There are very few saintly organizations in the world. Environmental groups have agendas. Their policy prescriptions differ from one another. They are contentious. They have interests. People in organizations have public and policy agendas which have lots of different motivations including their own desire to aggrandize their particular organization. I am involved in university politics, and I recognize it in myself. From an analytical point of view, the term "interest group" (I understand that the rhetoric of "special" interest groups has a negative connotation) is useful, and it is healthy to recognize that there are interests and agendas everywhere. To rhetorically cover that up by saying that there are interest groups and there are other nice civil society groups does not get us very far.

DAVID WELCH
Social Planning Council of Ottawa-Carleton and
University of Ottawa

We have to recognize that there are problems with the welfare state but it also has given us such things as bases for greater equality and a bit more hope for some people than we had previously. This statement does not detract from what has been said about the third sector or the voluntary sector. I agree with Al Hatton that we have to do things better, but I do not think it is the main problem today. The big problem is the downloading from the federal government to the provinces and the cutbacks of the provincial governments to the voluntary sector. A study in Ottawa demonstrated that there is no way the voluntary organizations can completely fill the vacuum. We are heading toward a situation of greater inequality. In a city like Ottawa, which is in a boom situation because of the high-tech industry, poverty is increasing. There are 15,000 people on the waiting list for social housing as a result of the "Silicone Valley" situation. The boom has caused rents to increase dramatically and a whole sector of society is excluded. It is important to understand where these people fit in as citizens. We can debate a lot in an academic forum but we are still excluding thousands of people from any meaningful participation in what we call civil society.

KEYNOTE ADDRESS

BEYOND THE BORDER: TWO VIEWS ON THE RELATIONSHIP BETWEEN THE THIRD SECTOR AND THE STATE FROM ABROAD

Chief Charity Commissioner of England and Wales John Stoker delivered the Friday evening keynote address to the conference on the state of the relationship between the voluntary sector and state in the United Kingdom. He responded to the ongoing debate in Canada over the idea of a Charity Commission by outlining the role and future of the British Commission, speaking frankly about some of his worries. While largely optimistic about the future of the commission, he forewarned his Canadian audience about some of the potential challenges facing them if the government and voluntary sector decide to create a Canadian version of the Charity Commission. He dabbled further in the Canadian debate by offering advice on legislative versus common law definitions of charity. It would behoove Canadians to heed his cautions.

Secretary General of CARE International Guy Tousignant took the audience further abroad with his address on the relationship between the state and the voluntary sector at the international level. Using CARE as a case study, he examined the possibilities of forging strong relationships between the nongovernmental organizations (NGOs), capturing some of the complications and opportunities embedded in those relationships. He hinted at the tensions in the democratization of international governance evoking comparisons with the difficulties being experienced domestically as the federal government and voluntary sector work toward a more inclusive policy process. He emphasized the positive aspect of relations, counselling NGOs to pay particular attention to their reputations as they engage in advocacy, lobbying, representation and raising public awareness. How an NGO conducts itself on any given issue will affect perceptions of its future legitimacy and thus its access to government.

JOHN STOKER
Chief Charity Commissioner
Charity Commission for England and Wales

A Charity Commission for Canada?

It is a pleasure to be here, partly because of the particularly exciting point that the debate on the future of the third sector has reached in Canada, and also because this conference marks the launch of a major initiative on public policy and the third sector by the School of Policy Studies here at Queen's University with the support of the Kahanoff Foundation. I would like to wish the School and the initiative well.

The first two panels of the conference were very interesting. Trying to achieve unanimity in the British voluntary sector has been compared to herding cats. In government and in the sector, as Susan Carter's talk highlighted, those planning change are going to have some challenges to handle. Arthur Drache, I thought, described even more pungently what working with government departments can sometimes be like for those in the voluntary sector. It is nice to see that some things are the same wherever you go. But, working with the third sector has taught me a healthy respect for its ability to work constructively while managing those wide differences in view that it has within itself. This is part of its strength and as well, it is also part of the fun of being a public servant working with the voluntary sector.

I am an outsider, but it looks to me as if Canadians have handled the debate about the future of the sector very impressively. I have been struck by the clarity of the analysis, by the confidence and open-mindedness shown in presenting the issues for public debate. In the sector's own Report of the Panel on Accountability and Governance in the Voluntary Sector (PAGV), the Government of Canada/Voluntary Sector Joint Table's Initiative and the Voluntary Sector Initiative to which they led, look like models of coherent consultation, partnership, and planning.

I am here to address how relations stand in the United Kingdom between the government and voluntary organizations, and how the Charity Commission plays its part. I will share some of the concerns that I have about my job in Britain. (It is inaccurate, I know, but I will use "British" for English and Welsh.) And then I would just like to have a bit of fun at the end by honing in on some of the issues that are live at the moment in the Canadian debate and giving you a British angle on them.

I am appointed by a minister but I am a politically neutral administrator in the British tradition. I am not affiliated to any political party. Among other things, what that means is that I have to be fairly careful in the terms in which I describe British government policies about the third sector. I will try and describe the politics clearly but definitely from the outside. That way, with a little luck, nobody should feel an overpowering urge to shoot me when I get home.

The first thing to say about charity in the UK is that it is very big and it is very old. How big? Well the charities that the commission regulates number 187,000. They have assets around about £65 billion sterling. That is more than $140 billion Canadian. Income is about £23 billion sterling or $50.8 billion Canadian. Since 1994 when the national lottery was introduced, it has produced an extra £10 billion sterling for good causes. And of that £10 billion about 40 percent has actually gone to bodies that are charities so it has been a golden age if you are a grant-seeking charity. The total figures for charities are even bigger because there are some that for legal reasons we do not actually regulate.

I said it was big and old. Well how old? I think the oldest charity that I actually know dates from the thirteenth century. It still exists as a charity and it is the successor of the fund that was set up to provide for London River crossings originally using toll income from the first London bridge.

Financially, this sector has a very funny shape though not that different in some respects to here. Out of those 187,000 charities, the biggest 300 account for our 40 percent of the resources. The biggest 3,000 account for over 90 percent of the resources. So at one end of the scale, we have a relatively few rich, professional organizations, and at the other we have a huge number of tiny ones and they are operating on slim resources. They run the governance as well as their operations wholly or mainly on volunteers' skills and time, and employ little in the way of staff. If you have a sector that is that funny shape and has those big numbers, a pretty obvious point that arises is that if it is your job to regulate it, then you cannot afford to be a control freak, you have to pick your targets.

The PAGV report talks about a lighter reporting regime for small charities defined as handling less than $200,000 in income. So small here is quite a relative term. The British arrangement is that annual reports and accounts have to be submitted to the commission by charities with more than £10,000, or C$22,000 in annual income or expenditure. The reporting requirements are simple at that level, with more complexity beginning at £100,000 and again at a quarter of a million. But those arrangements mean that while 45,000 charities are subject to the full monitoring regime, this is only about a quarter of the total of the sector in numbers of charities. Therefore, as a regulator we tend to target our resources to a considerable extent to the big charities because that is where the money is. Materiality makes sense. If you want to cover the whole patch on the same basis as those bigger ones, then that would obviously be very resource-intensive. You could not do it on the kind of resources that we consume at the moment. A related problem is that expectations about what the commission can actually do in the fields of intervention and maybe even more so in terms of prevention, are often unrealistic. I suggest that conditioning public expectations at the outset is an important opportunity for you as you set up your new system.

There was a lot of talk about partnership. For many years, governments in the UK have been increasingly interested in working in partnership with the third sector. Part of this has actually been about recognizing the voice of the community expressing itself directly rather than through the ballot box. I do not think that necessarily means that they are democratic in a better sense from elected institutions. It just means they are doing something different. Other factors have included concern over the size of the state and the proportion of national resources that it consumes. Governments of all colours have been looking for ways to reduce that. I think in Britain, but I detect not here, that search for ways to reduce the size of the state is now a part of the left-right consensus rather than a left-right issue. Part of that trend has involved looking outside the state sector for the devolved delivery of functions and services formally delivered directly by the state. In a variety of areas, personal care, training and education, and many others the voluntary sector has been better placed than the commercial sector to take up the slack as the state tries to shrink. And in some areas — in the provision of social housing in particular — the trend involves more than just delivery of services. It has actually included the transfer of quite substantial assets and activities from the public to the third sector.

That trend has given rise to a number of issues within the sector itself. One of these is whether the essential independence of the third sector can be preserved where parts of it deliver services increasingly as the agent of the state and do so under conditions that mean they are increasingly dependent on the state for their financial lifeblood. Whatever the answer to this, my own view is that what is described as the "contract culture" is fine provided that charities actually use it to deliver services that offer value and are in keeping with their mission for the public benefit. What is not okay is that charities are being used just for delivery and someone else sets the strategic priorities and calls the shots. What it must mean is that the state takes an increasing interest in the efficiency and the professional capability that the sector shows and the state looks to us in the commission to help promote the setting of standards and to foster improved performance by charities.

This trend toward partnership has been taken to an unprecedented level by the government since 1997. There is a lot of stress at the moment on the moral and civic value of volunteering itself. It has never really been so clearly recognized before in British mainstream politics and the government is actually working to a newly announced target of trying to find an extra one million volunteers by the year 2004. It has also set in place a framework of national and local compacts with the voluntary sector in order to provide a view of rights and obligations for each of the partners. There is an understanding on both sides that in principle this covers key areas including the basis on which financial relationships are handled between the governments and charities, grant finances or contract finances. It also includes clear understandings on entitlement to consultation and policy formation and a great many other things. I see, without great surprise, that the development of a not dissimilar accord is now underway here in Canada.

There is still an undertone of anxiety. The third sector in Britain, as here, values its right to dissent and to say when the emperor's clothes might be looking a little threadbare and transparent. Capture is definitely a worry. Charities like being able to go to number 11 Downing Street and "chew the fat" with the Chancellor of the Exchequer, but they are very concerned that when they return to their constituencies, they are seen still to be their own men and women. These are risks that they are prepared to manage in return for the kind of access that is available at the moment on the political front and the influence that comes with it.

Against that background and that sort of historical development I suppose you might call it, the Charity Commission acts as a regulator and as the enabler for charities. Both these strands are actually spelled out in the legislation. The overall aim that we express by providing active supervision for the charities sector, is to give the public confidence in the integrity of charities. Our statutory duties are to promote better standards of administration in charities, to give the trustees that run them the advice they need whether collectively or individually and to identify and deal with mismanagement and abuse. There is a rider that goes along with those functions in the legislation that says that whichever job we are doing, we must exercise all our functions so as best to ensure that charities' resources are applied effectively in pursuit of their charitable objects. This is important. It means in particular that we should always be thinking about the interests of beneficiaries of charities and not just about the niceties of the law and certainly not about the details of process. It also means that if things go right and we do the job properly, the outcome of what we do is going to be a charity that is back on track rather than closed down or punished or deregistered, especially where we are dealing with problems that have come up as a result of mismanagement rather than abuse.

We have 550 staff at the Charity Commission. I think they do an excellent job on the whole. They are mainly generalists, but they also include accountants and lawyers. We operate out of three sites: one in London, one in Liverpool up in the northwest of England, and one in the southwest (Taunton). Governance is by five commissioners, appointed by ministers but non-partisan experts recruited by an open process rather than by politicians. Two of us, myself and the head of our legal function, are executives. The other three are non-executive, bringing special skills and experience: one in charity law, one in accounting and finance, and one in wider voluntary sector activities and issues. The commissioners are appointed for terms between three and five years.

At the front end of the process dealing with new charities, the commission keeps the register of charities, not the tax authorities. We decide on about 8,000 to 9,000 applications each year against the common law on charitable status. For the last couple of years, details from the register have been available online on our Web site, and the growing use of information technology is definitely one direction where the commission sees its future as lying. I am not at all surprised either to see that part of the Canadian Voluntary Sector Initiative is the proposal for the development of a similar database.

In the process of charitable registration, if an applicant meets the legal criteria — that is, wherever its purposes are legally and exclusively charitable — then we have no discretion and we must and do register the applicant as a charity. But before we register it, we ask questions intended to check whether or not the organization is in good faith, and whether it has the financial and other capabilities to operate effectively. We check out the record of prospective trustees of new charities, especially where the charity will be operating in high-risk areas, including working with children. We are developing the commission's capacity for assessing risk at the point of registration, so that, for example, we can earmark new charities for special monitoring attention as they pass through into the system if we think that they need it.

The arrangements for monitoring charity accounts are quite new in their present form. They are based on a common framework for charity accounts which took its definitive form under the commission's leadership as recently as 1995. Prior to that, the monitoring of accounts was fairly variable. We are now coming to the end of only the third annual cycle of compulsory monitoring based on common accounting standards. Common accounting standards do not mean strict uniformity and comparability — as any accountants among you, and dare I say regulators as well, will certainly appreciate — but they do represent a quantum step forward since 1995 in the availability both to us and, through us, to the public of comprehensive and reasonably consistent information about charities: their finances and their governance. Every year some 45,000 sets of accounts are subject to computer auditing checks and possible causes for concern are examined. In 2000, about 12,000 charities triggered one of the indicators that suggested some cause for concern. Most of those could be investigated pretty easily from other information that the commission holds. But for about 1,300 charities we did need to contact the agencies and investigate. In addition to computer audits, the larger charities' accounts also receive a direct check by the commission's accountants.

The Charity Commission publishes a wide range of guidance for charity trustees and staff about all areas of the charity operation including governance and financial matters. This guidance is available on the Web site and on paper. We also advise trustees of individual charities on particular issues and we have powers that are similar to the powers of the courts to help trustees monitor and modernize their constitutions where they have become outdated and unviable. Where it is in the charity's interests, the commission can authorize one-off actions or transactions which would not normally be possible under a charity's constitution.

This support function adds up to a large part of the commission's enabling and support role. There is nothing particularly "pink and cuddly" about this support though. Although the commission is supposed to be helpful, usually its concern is to see that charities understand and observe core regulatory and legal requirements and other kinds of good practice. I suspect that this business of updating individual constitutions is maybe less of an issue here than it is in Britain given that the Canadian sector is by and large of more recent growth. But it is important in the British circumstances where, for example, charities were originally founded in the eighteenth century to provide material for petticoats for deserving virgins in particular towns and cities. For obvious reasons, the days are gone — no matter how hard you search — when you can find petticoat flannel. Wherever you find one of those examples, it means that there is good charitable resource that is sitting there doing nothing. If you can actually find analogous purposes and modernize a constitution it means that you can release funds for good purposes. In the case of the oldest charity, which was founded to keep up London's bridges, millions of pounds a year can now be spent on a wide range of analogous activities such as providing mobility for London's elderly and poorly off. But it is only able to do that because we worked with the trustees to modernize their arrangements and find analogous purposes for the surplus money.

Turning to mismanagement and abuse, we must realize that it is always going to happen. Reports and allegations come to the commission from a variety of external sources as well as from the monitoring and the checks that we do internally. When reports come in, there is always a preliminary evaluation of the evidence, which is a quick and cost-effective way to identify those cases where a formal investigation is needed and those where concerns are not well founded or where they can be dealt with by means of advice. A formal inquiry will normally be opened only where there may be a need for the commission's powers of intervention, such as the suspension or dismissal of trustees, or the freezing of accounts. It is obviously important that trustees who are getting into trouble should feel able to come to the commission for advice without fear of an oppressive response. But we will virtually always open an inquiry where there is evidence of fraud, serious maladministration or deliberate abuse. Every year we do about 1,200–1,300 evaluations. We carry about 200–250 full investigations. Staff conducting inquiries are skilled in interviewing techniques and acquiring evidence, and have a sound knowledge of charity law and accounts. They have professional support from the commission's lawyers and investigative accountants. They work closely with the police, other government departments including Inland Revenue and Customs and Excise, and other agencies and local authorities.

Our budget for this is approximately £21.5 million a year. By the end of the next financial year, this amount will have held level in cash terms for six years. That has not been easy. But the government has agreed to increase our resources by some 20 percent at the end of this period. This is going to allow us to do some new things, as well as more and better of some existing things that we do. This was a new experience for me. I submitted my bid in February for a number of new things, which I will describe later. Normally what happens is that you think of a number and double it and the Treasury thinks of a number and halves it in a good year. In a bad year what they do is say, "Ah well, that is all very interesting. Let's ask him what he would do if we took 10 percent off what he has got now?" But I received a letter from the Chief Secretary of the Treasury, who is the minister who looks after the public expenditure and negotiations, which said, "Dear John, subject to the technicalities I agree with your bid." So I have taken that home and I am going to frame it and hang it up. It is a collector's item. You do not get letters like that from the chief secretary twice in a lifetime!

That money is important to us. First, subject to a detailed investment case which is with the Treasury now, it will allow us to upgrade our information technology systems. This will allow us to move toward our target of being able to conduct our business electronically with anyone who wants it that way, and it will have serious helpful spinoffs for our capacity to use this technology to make information about charities widely and easily available. Second, we plan to double our visiting program to charities from about 300 to 600 a year, and to overhaul their targeting, planning, execution, and follow-up. The idea is to increase significantly their impact as a regulatory tool, as well as to help our relationship grow with the sector and enhance our ability to monitor developing trends and issues to spot problems and act on them quickly. Third, we are planning to develop the capacity to carry out and publish fieldwork that looks at cross-cutting themes and issues inside the sector. These would be similar to some of the cross-cutting issues and studies that a number of British national audit bodies publish on the public sector at the moment. These will give a new dimension to our ability to monitor the sector — to sharpen our view of what actually happens out there, to highlight good and "less good" practices, and to encourage the one and discourage the other. I see this initiative as part of the commission's growth as an organization that deploys influence and moral authority alongside its legal powers. Finally, we intend to increase our capacity for regulatory inquiries into individual charities by more than 20 percent. This reflects our view, which is widely shared in Britain including the charity sector, that a sharp edge to the commission's supervision and compliance activities must be good for public confidence in the integrity of charity.

What about the less comfortable parts of the picture? Are there any things that keep me awake at night about the job? Well, yes, there are actually. It is fashionable at the moment to see the management of anything pretty much — public, private or voluntary — in terms of risk. It is actually a good model for the charitable sector in Britain and, therefore, for us in the commission. There is no doubt that there are risks to charities, that they are growing and that the rate of growth in the number and seriousness of the risk is actually accelerating. Some of them are risks to the reputation of charities.

A few of these risks deserve mention. Some are risks to reputation. A major abuse or fraud in just one, high profile charity can have big knock-on effects for charities as a whole. You can also get damage done by abuse in small charities where it attracts widespread attention. This is a particular problem for the commission as regulator. While it makes sense to concentrate our resources on the "big boys" who account for the lion's share of the money, the strategy for supervision is to deal with problems when they occur at the high-volume, low-resource end of the sector as well. With 187,000 charities, you cannot have all the bases covered all the time. As a result, I sometimes lie awake and wonder how much I do not know, particularly in that very big area of the sector of the small charities where we do not do the full monitoring regime, and I constantly wonder whether we have the balance of resources and activities right across the sector.

There are, of course, risks to reputation that have nothing to do with abuse. Some of them simply relate to efficiency. Market research in Britain shows that a majority of the British public think that there are simply too many charities. And the most common, unprompted concern about charities that people express in surveys is that administrative costs take up too much of their income. In fact, people think that the proportion is on average a lot higher than it is but it is interesting that they should think that. There are two parts to the solution here. One is simply that charities, like businesses and regulators, must look for continuous improvements in value for money and they do that by developing their management competence and by bearing down on costs. This is especially true of the bigger charities which are professionally resourced and not wholly volunteer-run. The other part of the solution is that British charities do need to become better at communications. In particular, they need to be able to persuade their stakeholders in the public that the good they do in the real world is solid, visible, and worth the costs. The more that charities succeed in actually shifting the debate away from the size of overheads and onto what they deliver for their beneficiaries and the value that represents, the better it is going to be for all of us and the more people are going to be prepared to get involved and to give. In Britain, there is still a ways to go before communications and the necessary standards have been achieved.

Fundraising is another big reputational risk. British charities, for example, do a lot of fundraising mailouts. Often there is not always the difference in quality and ethos of this charity material from the promotional materials from commercial enterprises that hit the mailboxes at the same time. The result is a risk that the public's trust in what charities tell them about the world and what they do in it might be reduced. There are some signs from market research that this may be happening. Cold-calling on the phone, for example, and face-to-face relationship marketing type techniques are growing in scale in Britain and they add to this fundraising risk. For example, in the surveys that we do,

85 percent of people said that they positively disliked being cold-called by charities and yet a lot of charities do it.

Raising money is too important to be left to the fundraising professionals. It must be the trustees who exercise effective control and who are sensitive to the impact that activities have on the public. We also need a bit of growth in responsible and effective self-regulation by the British fundraising profession. This has actually begun this past year. We have the first sort of statement of principles that can be written on a mouse pad or a postcard and pinned above a desk. We have had lots of technical advice about different techniques before, but for the first time we are starting to hone in on the ethics. This is good. Licensing fundraisers, as you do in Canada, gives a completely different kind of control and I can see why you do it. However, it would be very much against the current trend in Britain, which is for a lighter, rather than a heavier, touch for regulation in society as a whole.

Apart from reputation of risks, there is a competitive risk that charities face. People think there are too many charities, and public giving to charities, though the trend has now bottomed out, has declined significantly from an all-time peak in the early 1990s. Part of the answer here is that appropriate competition is a good thing: it drives excellence and greater competence. Some charities, not for the most part the very biggest, are not as attentive as they should be to the need for continuous improvement. This is going to be one of the keys to survival in circumstances where charities are competing more and more for their funds.

The sector also needs to develop better ways to rationalize the best way to improve delivery to beneficiaries. For example, the client base for many ex-servicemen's and servicewomen's charities will halve over the next decade or two as the numbers who were subject to compulsory military service fall. It is very difficult sometimes for charities, but the consciousness of the need for rationalization is growing and the solutions have to come from the sector. I am glad about this growing awareness and the imagination and energy that many charities are putting into the search for solutions, since the commission must not impose solutions by command and control. Sometimes, the answer will be closure or merger. Some charities may have a life-span like other things and there is nothing wrong with that, painful though the realization may be. More often, the answer needs to be better coordination and wider reliance on partnership in charity operations. This is particularly so in those areas — children, animal, and cancer charities — where the popular perception of "too many charities" may perhaps have most substance.

Next, there is a demographic risk in the UK. All the figures seem to show us that the generation under 25 years old is much less willing than its predecessors were to get involved either as donors or as volunteers. This may be linked to wider trends in consumer expectations. It is surely linked in some way to the fact that this generation is the first to have truly grown up in the Global Village of which the Internet is the greatest manifestation. The public policy emphasis on the value of volunteering that we currently have in Britain is part of the response to this; Internet software solutions to match people to volunteering needs and opportunities are another. But charities also need to recognize the demographic threat, and to look for ways for each charity individually to reach out effectively to young people at the grassroots level.

This leads naturally on to technological risk. Even some quite substantial British charities seem to think that embracing modern information and communications technology is optional for them. It is not. Nor is it for quite small charities. There is a wake up call here. If you are a charity that thinks that it does not have to invest in a PC and thinks a Web site is where the cobwebs haven't been swept away, you need to wake up and join the twenty-first century, you will not survive.

Next, there is some governance risk. Charities depend upon volunteers to govern as well as to deliver charity operations. The model of having a body of trustees who within some basic legal rules are entirely self-governing and accountable to no one for their decisions is a pretty unusual one in an age where discharging public functions usually feels more like it is about accountability and responsibility than it is about the exercise of power, as in the past. That is a trend to which charities are not immune. The key, perhaps, is that the majority of trustees are not paid. While this continues — and there is some pressure for change — the system will probably stay robust. But only if the public's and beneficiaries' desire for, and entitlement to, information and full transparency are embraced and met. Also, at the moment, many charity trustees are older rather than younger and more rather than less prosperous. This is not surprising, older people often have more time and money, and we want the older generation to be actively involved. But we also need to find ways of making trusteeship open to younger people, to the employed, to the less prosperous, to a wider ethnic and social mix. To encourage this, we have recently published advice designed to make it easier to have beneficiaries and their interests represented on charities' governing bodies.

Finally, there is what I might call the millennial risk. A system based on common law concepts like equity and precedent rather than codification and legislative decision has virtues but it is bound to come under question in an age when people are looking for simplicity, certainty, and transparency and they think a great deal about citizens' entitlements. This really is the area of risk that we manage at the commission. The answer is to modernize to the greatest extent the system allows. In the commission we try to do this wherever the opportunity arises. We do it by constantly keeping interpretations of charity law — which we cannot fundamentally change — under review. This has led us to recognize new charitable purposes such as urban and rural regeneration and the relief of unemployment. We have consulted on proposals to do the same in relation to community capacity-building and to environmental conservation. We can do it by giving a lead on identifying changes and trends in the environment in which charities operate and encouraging and advising on ways for charities to adapt. We do it also by responding to the growing demands for accountability and transparency in relation to charities' activities, and using the new technology — and encouraging charities themselves to use it — to make more and even better information publicly available. We also do it by trying always to find clear and helpful language, expressed with a human face, to interpret a complex system in ways that the people who actually run charities will find serviceable and user-friendly.

Now, this is the fun bit for me, sticking my nose just a little bit into some of the issues about the future for your Canadian system. First, who should decide what is charitable and what is not? The PAGV report is quite clear about that: it should be Canada's Parliament and not the courts. There is a great deal to be said in support of this approach in principle: it is democratic; it allows you to target the special status that comes with charitable status and the resources that the community provides via the state; and it has the virtue of greater clarity — provided that the drafting challenges can be surmounted and new anomalies avoided. Think about a statutory definition of religion, for example. This approach might help to dovetail charitable and non-charitable activities in a "charity plus" approach to supporting and supervising the voluntary sector of the kind Arthur Drache described.

The contrary view that the courts should decide is often argued in Britain, mainly because any statutory list would exclude as well as include. Those who argue from this point of view see common law charitable status as a citizen's entitlement, accrued and guaranteed over the years through decisions by the courts which are also accountable. A lot of people in Britain agree. They see citizens as having a right for their charitable activities to be legally recognized, and a right not to be taxed on what they do voluntarily for the public good. I am not expressing a personal view here, still less a Charity Commission one. But the PAGV panel assertion was so strong that I felt the urge to look at the other side of the argument. I should perhaps just say before moving on that we in Britain maybe see the common law a bit differently than Canadians because you have a written constitution and we do not. The Charity Commission does seem to be able to interpret and develop it more than Arthur described the courts as doing here.

Next, what do you do about enforcement? Well, enforcement of what and in compliance with what? And here I was quite interested to read the documents that came out last year because I suspect that the kind of preferred models that those reports of the panel and the joint tables discuss may be very different from what we actually do in the Charity Commission. The stress there is very much on compliance with legal rules and particularly with the *Income Tax Act*. In Britain, the commission does not police charities' tax affairs, though it often works closely with the tax authorities. On tax matters, charities deal directly with the tax departments. The commission's role is much wider since we try to ensure that charities actually comply with their own constitutions. The logic is that charities have been given their resources for a specific purpose whether it is by endowment or by public contribution, and public confidence demands that someone ensures that charities stick by the agreement that this implies. You may end up with very different results if you decide to give this responsibility to a new commission with mainly "coaching" functions, or to the tax authorities, or if you decide, as it seems you might, not to regulate it closely at all.

How will the system handle charities that are troubled without actually being abusive or incompetent? The PAGV report suggested that a commission could investigate public complaints and that its first role would be to solve any problems in a constructive manner. Now, if I were you I would not underestimate what this might involve. Most people running charities can and do their jobs. They get along with each other. But unless human nature is different here, you are going to get some disagreements within the charities and between people running charities and their beneficiaries. Those disagreements are going to be bitter and intractable at times. Facts as well as merits will be disputed. People involved will not let go and will not compromise. You will need to be very clear on your approach: what issues that a coaching commission will get involved in and what it will not. The better you define the limits of regulation and the more effectively you condition expectations, the more trouble you will save later on. But if you decide that you want to engage in mediation and coaching on a large scale, you will not do it with an organization of 100 staff.

The limits of regulation also matter in relation to advice to voluntary bodies about improved governance and wider operational best practice. The model that we in England and Wales are increasingly working toward does see the lead on promotion of good practice as a matter of partnership. Issues would fall most naturally to the commission where a core regulatory interest is at stake, and to the sector itself, acting collectively, where the issue is simply how to do business professionally, effectively, and economically. Again, in Canada you have a valuable opportunity to clarify the deal at the outset as you develop a new system. It is not surprising that transparency and accountability have figured largely in the Canadian debate but it came as a bit of a surprise to me to realize the strength of the Canadian tradition of treating charitable status mainly as a tax matter. The restrictions placed on the options of the regulators to make information publicly available, especially when things have gone wrong, from British experience does feel out of tune with the age. So too does having charitable status decided by the tax authorities.

The report of the joint tables correctly states that publicity is quite a powerful item in the regulator's toolbox. It is a fair comment that the joint tables recommend care in its use. Does highlighting intervention where things have gone wrong produce more harm than good? My own view is that regulation cannot enhance confidence if it is invisible. Of course, it is always essential to act fairly, whether in cop mode or coach mode. But, for example, while the commission has power to publicize the results of its investigations of mismanagement and abuse, it has very rarely done so. From now on, it will be publishing investigative reports on its Web site. Too few charities in Britain have been as prompt as the law requires in submitting their annual reports and accounts. We have plans to "name and shame" persistent offenders among larger charities. That is where there is most public interest in transparency and least excuse for non-compliance.

Other sanctions against charities have been another important issue in the Canadian debate. I wish the Joint Regulatory Table the best of luck in its further work on this delicate area. Curiously, the main sanction available in Canada — deregistration — is not available in the UK on the same basis. Perhaps it ought to be, though the decision to make any change would be for legislators and not the commission. Fines as a sanction have little appeal where the result would be to take money from charity funds and transfer it to the Treasury, and I see that the Canadian debate has reflected this. In Britain, we have a number of other sanctions available where misconduct or mismanagement may be involved. These include freezing accounts, suspending or removing trustees, and appointing a temporary manager to administer the charity in the place of the trustees. All of these can be pretty useful on occasion, and the range of options available allows us to tailor our approach to the needs of particular cases.

Finally, I would just like to stress again what I think is probably the central point to bear in mind as you think about a new system for charity in Canada. This is that the system for deciding charitable status must be able to accommodate change and to adapt to developments in social and economic circumstances and attitudes. It has got to be a system that must be able to accommodate change. There is a debate about whether or not the common law could do that. Would statutory definition be any different? Can you get one that is sufficiently clear and unambiguous? A good way to check that out is to derive your own personal definition of religion, then check it out against the whole range of what some people might think of as religion. It may not be entirely straightforward. Statutory definition is also subject to rigidities simply because you cannot change the interpretation of it in the same way as you can the common law to accommodate developing economic and social views. I do think that adaptation to change is the key. Our British experience shows that the common law system can be operated that way. Whichever way you do it, change is critical. The concept of charity has to live and grow if it is to survive.

GUY TOUSIGNANT
Secretary-General
CARE International

Making the Relationship Work: A View from the International Forum

I have sensed that the relationship between government and nongovernmental organizations (NGOs) tends to be perceived as a choice between state dominance and third sector dominance. In the international community, the NGO sector could tell many stories about the imperious power of the state, while on the other hand, governments could tell as many stories about the interference of NGOs in state affairs. However, in most countries of the world, this relationship contains many elements of cooperation and is, indeed, complementary.

I bring to this discussion my point of view as secretary-general of CARE International, a worldwide confederation of nonprofit and nongovernmental organizations. I bring my experience in the field, both as a military person and as a humanitarian. I am a retired General from the Canadian Armed Forces, an occupation that is not and should not be identified as a third sector of society anywhere around the world. My experience in the field of humanitarian work began in Africa, working for the United Nations as an Assistant Secretary-General/Force Commander responsible for the humanitarian response to the crisis in Rwanda. Slightly more than three years ago, I joined CARE as its secretary-general and, like most bureaucrats, the majority of my work is performed from my office in Brussels. I have, nonetheless, travelled to more than 80 countries around the world, including many where I have had the opportunity to go out into the field to observe the work of CARE. Like directors of most NGOs, I have attended many conferences with the UN, the World Bank, and civil societies where we regularly share our different experiences. Currently, I am the chairman of the Standing Committee of Humanitarian Response, which allows me the opportunity to meet with the heads of the other main humanitarian agencies such as the Red Cross, Médecins sans frontières, and Oxfam twice a year. I was in Mali observing the sort of relationship enjoyed by CARE and the Government of Mali and I will refer to that experience here. That is what I bring to the debate.

I will refer a great deal to CARE not because I want to promote the agency, but because it is a large NGO and I am most familiar with it. CARE also compares quite favourably with other NGOs. I discuss Mali not because it is our largest mission. To the contrary, it is more or less an average mission alongside the various missions that we have around the world. My objectives here will be to: (i) explain the type of relations a government might be willing to develop with nonprofit and nongovernmental organizations; (ii) explain the type of relations that an international organization such as CARE has with governments and international institutions; and (iii) touch on what the difficulties and challenges are for both governments and NGOs alike. I will provide some concrete examples of these points.

CARE is one of the largest NGOs in the world. Over the past 50 years, following its first humanitarian interventions in Central Europe, it has provided development and humanitarian support in all parts of the globe. Today, CARE is working in more than 70 countries. As with any NGO, CARE has developed sound connections with national governments of the industrialized world, but it also enjoys varied relationships with host governments where it operates. CARE International has also developed strong relations with international institutions such as the UN, the World Bank, and the European Union.

Because the last few decades have been so overwhelming in terms of the demands put on the humanitarian community, CARE has had to undertake the task of redefining its vision and mission. As a result of this rationalization process, CARE International's mission statement reads:

> To serve individuals and families in the poorest communities in the world. Drawing strength from our global diversity, resources and experiences, we promote innovative solutions and are advocates of global responsibility. We facilitate lasting change by:
>
> * strengthening capacity for self-help;
> * providing economic opportunity;
> * delivering relief in emergencies;
> * influencing policy decisions at all levels; and
> * addressing discrimination in all its forms

It is not the first time that CARE has had to review its mission and its vision. As a matter of fact, I believe that this is the fifth time in its history that CARE has re-assessed how it can have the greatest impact on those in need. But it is important to know what an NGO like CARE does if we want to understand that (for us) success in development work is directly linked to the quality of relations we maintain with local governing institutions.

We no longer give "CARE Packages" (that may not mean too much to some of you, but it is a bit of an icon for others) that contain food, blankets, pots and pans, etc., except when we are involved in an emergency situation. As a matter of fact, there is ample evidence that simple donations do very little to bring about lasting change to poor nations and, on the contrary, can have a negative impact on beneficiaries. Over the years, we have learned that sustainable development stands a much better chance of success if people are provided with knowledge and the basic tools to change their living conditions. That approach certainly goes a long way toward respecting human dignity among the very poor communities.

In its approach to development in the Third World, CARE would be unable to accomplish lasting change on its own. Strengthening capacity for self-help, providing economic opportunity, influencing policy decisions at all levels, and addressing discrimination in all its forms implies strong partnership with a multitude of actors. Our work is only possible because we have decided to collaborate, coordinate, and partner with the main players in development and the humanitarian sectors. Those actors or players are:

- the beneficiaries themselves;
- the government of the developing countries and the civil society (organizations of citizens, NGOs, churches, trade unions, etc.);
- private international or national companies;
- other international NGOs (we have a lot of partnerships with bigger, international NGOs such as Oxfam and Save the Children);
- international multilateral institutions (UN, World Bank, European Commission); and
- the government of supporting countries like Canada and the civil society of those countries.

How CARE International articulates these partnership relations varies a great deal depending on where we have programs established and the different partners we are trying to work with. Obviously, we have a better relationship at the moment with Mali than we would have with Sierra Leone. I will focus here on how we approach our relations with governments and international multilateral institutions.

Although it would be inaccurate to say that all NGOs think alike, it would be fair to say that the NGO community agrees on why governments or multilateral organizations should be interested in collaborating and forming partnerships with NGOs. I make a distinction here between collaboration and partnership because certain NGOs will reject any form of partnership while they will promote some forms of collaboration. That said, CARE would not hesitate to point out to future partners that nonprofit organizations offer several comparative advantages such as: (i) independence; (ii) flexibility; (iii) access to information; (iv) inexpensive (as a rule); (v) operate in a spirit of solidarity; (vi) innovation; and (vii) mobilization of public opinion. Let me elaborate on those things. As organizations of private rights, NGOs are not directly subjected to government policies and, likewise, to political, commercial and military ambitions. Independence means that NGOs can work in situations and places where governments are unable to intervene for political and diplomatic reasons. NGOs also have a faster perception of environmental changes and adapt easily to them. In addition, NGOs have access not only to official information but also to other proper sources of information because of national and international NGO networks, among other things. Another comparative advantage is that NGOs tend to limit their non-operational costs. Therefore, governments have an economic interest to employ NGOs for short-term programs.

To re-enforce the last two examples of comparative advantages, let me simply point out the long presence of CARE in some countries and the high percentage of local staff in the CARE country offices. We have had programs in

Bangladesh and Mali for more than 25 years and in India for 50 years. In Bangladesh, CARE employs more than 2,000 individuals and 98 percent of the staff are local people who have been trained. That percentage of local staff in relation to international staff is the norm with CARE.

NGOs also strive to offer services according to beneficiary needs and their personnel are motivated by a sense of philanthropy and solidarity. Ambition and lucrative interests are rare among NGOs working in the field. Paying attention to beneficiaries' preferences and interests is an accepted best-practice by the NGO community today. Very few projects, including the ones that I recently observed in Mali, are begun without the full agreement of all locally concerned parties. In addition, CARE does not negotiate these agreements. Instead, CARE will teach local institutions how to work together and arrive at a mutually agreed course of action.

Another advantage is that NGOs also have the capacity to sharpen and influence public opinion and to promote the defence of public causes (promotion of human rights, ecological matters, and so on). Let me give you an example of this. Consider, for instance, the plight of the starving people of Sudan in 1998. The NGO community was instrumental in sharpening and influencing public opinion on the forgotten war in Sudan. It has been going on for 22 years and very few people know about it. Many people know about the famine. In the last decade, of all the other conflicts combined, more people have died in Sudan as a result of the war. The NGOs were the ones who made it known, consider the role that CARE and its federation of ten members played in this. CARE Canada was established in 1946 and enjoys a very good reputation here. CARE USA, the founding CARE in 1945, enjoys relationships with all sorts of organizations and has an excellent relationship with CML. CARE UK is one of our strongest in Europe. CARE Australia is the only operative NGO in the country. Other organizations are CARE Japan in Tokyo, CARE Germany, CARE Austria, CARE France, CARE Denmark, and CARE Norway. Together, they are a force not to be ignored. In the case of the Sudan, the unified message of CARE was very strong. This is the comparative advantage of an NGO with a world network. In addition, I would like to add that the NGO sector has substantially increased its capacity over the years. It includes professional bodies with strict quality control standards.

For all these reasons, governments and multilateral institutions should be interested in cooperating with NGOs. They are interested, for the most part, especially when NGOs are not seen as impinging on their responsibilities or viewed as direct competition. This cooperation would normally range from NGOs contributing to project and program management to contributions to policy dialogue and delivery. An example would be the current project in Mali that operates on the Niger River and inland delta and is intended to increase the productivity of 30,000 hectares of irrigated rice fields through a combination of improved management and improved control of flood waters. It affects 6,000 farmers in Europe. Every year the population of Mali depends on the Niger River to flood and then they plant rice and the waters then recede into the river. There is a critical time to do this or everything is lost. CARE, in cooperation with other NGOs, examined ways to improve the productivity and limit the risk of having a non-crop year. Through some engineering studies, they decided that they could construct dykes and actually retain the water a little longer and then when it had done its work, just let it go back into the Niger River. Through these changes, we doubled the production of rice in Mali.

I use this as an example of project and program management where the cooperation of all the institutions involved is needed. This project affected three groups of people. Obviously the farmers were very impressed with the new technology, which was very effective. But the herders who need the land and fishers who depend upon the Niger River were not as pleased. So what do we do for all three sectors? Here is the benefit of NGOs being able to work with the local community and associations, in this case the association of fishermen, the association of herders and farmers. Through discussions, they finally decided that the project made a lot of sense and found a common solution. Fishers were responsible for operating the dykes. When I was there at the end of the rainy season, the experts from CARE were telling me that the fishers might have opened the dykes too soon, but the local fishers managed the dykes and seemed to understand the local conditions. The fishers were catching fish as soon as they opened the dykes. Rice was plentiful. For the first time Mali will have a surplus production and they will be able to export it.

Now where is Mali? It is south of the Sahara Desert, Nigeria on the east, Senegal and Mauritania on the west, and the Ivory Coast on the south. The population is approximately 10,000,000 people with a birthrate of 2.2 percent and a mortality rate of about 128 per 1,000 births and about 500 per 1,000 before the age of 5. This is high for Africa. The life expectancy of 54 years compares favourably with other countries. It has a very harsh environment: one day it is a desert and the next produces some greenery. There are no natural resources. People depend on cotton and the production of rice and fish to survive. Mali is stable and since it has no natural resources it is of no strategic importance. And yet, a lot of people need help. The gross domestic product is $580 a year — less than $2 a day. That is what they have to survive on and that is why we are there.

Mali is a useful example of how NGOs contribute to policy dialogue and delivery. The Government of Mali is in the process of decentralization. And that means that suddenly they have elected mayors in the various communities, regional governments, and some provincial governments. However, 28 percent of the people live in urban conditions, and in rural areas few people can read and write and many have less than a grade 2 education. It is fine to be elected mayor, but what does a mayor do? This is where the NGOs are involved, working with the local communities and providing them with the tools and the knowledge of responsibilities. For example, the local mayor who used to be the chief in one area, criticized our work and told us to ask the district commissioner to open the dyke because they did not have enough water. I was surprised by the people working in the field who told him to go to the district commissioner directly as the representative of the people. Before we left, he wanted us to have dinner with him because he was worried that he had insulted us. The point here is that the message is getting through. People are working at it, they are learning and learning quickly and they are very enthusiastic about it. It is not just at the local level. The president of Mali insisted that I spend an hour and a half with him while I was there so that he could express his gratitude for what the NGOs are doing and the types of partnerships we have helped create as well as for assistance with decentralization.

I recognize that in my example of Mali, I emphasized activities that were related to the joint implementation of programs. In such a scenario, I could easily portray NGOs as merely instruments of governments or as subcontractors. That would be so unmerited that I must now clarify the type of relationship NGOs seek to maintain with governments. It is true that the more we accept donations from governments, the more we are at risk of losing our own independence, and therefore, that would explain why most reputable NGOs will not accept more than a certain percentage of their total income from governments or multilateral donors. CARE does not have a stated policy to that effect but NGOs like OXFAM do. However, CARE will refuse projects and money with conditions that do not correspond to our strategic development strategy in a given country or do not meet our values and the beneficiaries' aspirations.

For us, the best type of partnership with governments and multilateral institutions would fall into four main categories: (i) advocacy; (ii) lobbying; (iii) representation; and (iv) raising public awareness. Advocacy, as we define it resides "in the dissemination of persuasive information, on behalf of/or in partnership with our 'clients' in developing countries, to those in a position to influence, make or carry out public policy decision." Our audience would include multilateral institutions (e.g., the UN or the World Bank), governments and bilateral donors and host governments. Our lobbying interventions, on the other hand, will reside in influencing policymakers for funding shifts or higher levels of financial support. For example, we have lobbied in the European Community to ask the Parliament and Commission not to shift all the money for the south to the east. Representation involves maintaining and strengthening relationships with government officials, the donor community, and other NGOs, as we do in our office in Geneva. Raising public awareness involves disseminating information in order to raise our profile or visibility and the plight of our beneficiaries.

These four ideas are closely linked. If you undertake advocacy activities for instance, and if your advocacy is done well, inevitably awareness about activities will be raised. If there is some representation, then maybe this will result in a shift of funding. The weight given to those areas will send a clear signal about who you are and what you intend to accomplish. For example, Amnesty International and the Red Cross, because of their size, are evenly involved in the four areas. In the case of CARE, it is only recently that we made the decision to develop our capacity to do advocacy work. Even today, our advocacy interventions are selective and tend to be targeted. For CARE, advocacy work needs to be clearly defined and must be seen as a tool to accomplish our mission, and not the mission itself. Therefore, we insist that CARE's advocacy work be rooted in its program experience and that it be carried out only selectively in order to maintain our credibility on very specific policy issues. I should also add that CARE's advocacy style tends to be pragmatic, down-to-earth, and non-confrontational. The highest priority is given to policy objectives that draw heavily on our field experience and are likely to have a significant impact on the poor communities we serve.

This will give you an example of what CARE does in that regard. I have had the pleasure of briefing the Security Council twice. The Council has only allowed NGOs to brief them three times. We were invited to discuss the protection of victims of conflicts and this is due to the type of relationship that we have with the Government of Canada and the Canadian ambassador. For that privilege, NGOs have to act in a very responsible way. In order for NGOs to have an impact, the message must be clearly focused on specific issues.

The second intervention was in Sudan in 1998. Care decided to make an assessment of what was happening in Sudan as the result of the famine. We had just saved 70,000 people in a small village and they were at level two of recovery when war broke out. If we were to stop feeding them, they would go back to their village and die. The question was asked: "How often do we have to save the same people?" There was no real famine here. It was a war. People were being used as human shields. So CARE decided to tell the government and also to tell the rebel forces that we were seriously considering pulling out of Sudan. It was audacious on our part to go to Khartoum and ask for an interview with government officials at the highest level, after the Americans had just bombed Khartoum, "You must stop this war. You must get behind the peace process and you must extend the ceasefire. Otherwise, the 70,000 people we just saved are going to die. And if you let that happen, we are pulling out. And on top of that the Security Council has agreed to listen to our message, so we are leaving here and we are going to New York to tell them the same thing." Surprisingly they listened and said, "You have earned the right to say something. You have been here a long time." We then went to talk to the rebel forces, not knowing how we would be received. The rebels in the south insisted that we give them at least five more minutes than we gave the governor and they wanted to listen to the message. We were then bold enough to go to President Morin of Kenya and ask him for his leadership in bringing people to the table. We met with the American ambassador and he said, "You have a vital interest here and you can contribute to peace." We presented our message to the Security Council. It was a consortium. Médecins sans Frontières joined us and Oxfam and perhaps for the first time, we all agreed on a single message — not easy in the NGO world. But it had an impact. Perhaps our effort contributed to the extension of the ceasefire. The war is not over, and CARE has left because of what was happening in the south. Still, it is possible to do effective advocacy work. Partnership can be formed with governments and international institutions. The message can be very powerful if it is well targeted and well done.

I have described a very positive situation where governments and NGOs work in perfect harmony. Unfortunately, the reality is somewhat different and cooperation between governments, multilateral institutions, and NGOs is not always easy. However, I refuse to dwell on examples of past failures and there are plenty of others who will provide you with a wealth of literature on what does not work in partnerships between governments and the third sector. I believe that it is far more useful to try to understand why so often there are severe misunderstandings and a great unwillingness from the two sides to collaborate with each other. On the one hand, NGOs are afraid of losing their independence and neutrality if they partner with government. They are afraid of becoming service providers or agents of a political body. On the other hand, governments and public bodies are afraid of any interference from the outside. They are afraid of losing credibility if they partner with the outside.

We know that the conditions for sustainable development require strong collaboration between all partners. There is no way to step backward on this. The major challenge for all of us is to make sure that there is nothing that can interfere in our relationships. How can we do that? Well, at the risk of sounding too simplistic:

- by knowing each other;
- by talking to each other;
- by communicating our priorities, objectives, vision and mission;
- by accepting our differences of opinion;
- by establishing the framework of our cooperation from the very beginning;
- by listening to the one we want to serve; and
- by looking toward the future and not at the daily constraints.

We all have a responsibility in making this relationship work. Events like this conference help to overcome the "us and them" attitude that is so widespread and damaging for effective cooperation. Hopefully in the future we will continue to use the constructive and collaborative pronoun "We." Together, We can make the changes that matter.

PANEL THREE

LEARNING ACROSS THE PROVINCES

TERRY GOERTZEN
Special Advisor
Minister of Health, Manitoba Government

Being Heard and Hearing: Communications Strategies from the Third Sector, Municipal and Provincial Government Perspectives

I want to begin with a personal note about my participation at the conference. As a special advisor to the minister of health, I have the privilege every day of sitting in a room where decisions are made about policy, about strategy, and about communications where people's lives are at stake and I give advice about what I think is the best course for the minister. I have been a civil servant at City Hall and I have also served and am serving in the third sector. Recently, I have been appointed to two nonprofit arts boards in Winnipeg: the Symphony and the Manitoba Theatre Centre. So I speak to you today as someone who has worked on both sides of the sector street. I receive my paycheck from serving in a government sector, but my passion comes from the third sector.

I would like to discuss being heard and hearing: communication strategies in the third sector as well as the provincial and municipal sectors. I plan to focus on communication strategies and their importance, but I do want to highlight some of the interesting facts about the voluntary sector in Manitoba. I want to acknowledge the current research being done by the intersectoral secretariat on voluntary sector sustainability in Manitoba. Sid Frankel and the secretariat have done some very innovative work, taking a distinctly Manitoban approach by including the government sector early, leading the discussion with government, and building from the bottom up.

Here are some of the key factors they have compiled about Manitoba. The province is a primary funder of many voluntary sector organizations; over 8,000 voluntary organizations with revenues totalling $4.5 million. According to 1997 data, 40 percent of Manitobans who are 15 years and older volunteer their time. At an average of 130 hours per year per volunteer the secretariat calculates that volunteers in Manitoba contribute over 44 million hours and over half a billion dollars to Manitoba's economy and quality of life each year. Manitoba has some great success stories when it comes to the third sector: the PanAm games, the large festivals with the volunteers who are involved, and, of course, our victory over the famous flood of 1997. Manitobans have consistently demonstrated a spirit of volunteerism and pulling together. Against this backdrop the secretariat has defined its challenge in Manitoba as follows. The voluntary sector is entering the twenty-first century facing a variety of challenges to the leadership of organizations and groups and, most importantly, limitations in securing the volunteers, staff, managerial talent, and financial resources to meet long-term community needs.

So when the third sector encounters governments, both municipal and provincial, they hear a familiar refrain to the one echoed across the country. Budgets are limited. Decreasing the tax burden is a priority. Somehow governments are attempting to reconcile fiscal prudence with higher than ever expectations about the quality of services citizens receive. These are the same citizens for whom the third sector is also advocating.

So within this cacophony of voices, how does the third sector get heard and how do governments listen? Implicit in the question then, in my experience, is the acknowledgement of the significance of communications for the third sector and indeed for all public life. In an era of sound bytes and focus groups we need to recover a sense of the significance, the true importance of communications. We forget in this cynical age that for centuries communications as a practice of rhetoric was regarded as the essential public art. It was Francis Bacon who said, "Histories make men wise; poets, witty; the mathematics, subtle; natural philosophy, deep; moral, grave; logic and rhetoric, able to contend." It is this ability that both the third sector and governments are constantly seeking — the ability to contend. This is what good communication is in the third sector and governments; and in the next 36 days,[1] we will probably hear a whole lot of rhetoric.

---

[1]Anticipating a federal election call.

I am going to suggest, based on my experience in the third sector, that one of the key communication strategies that fosters the ability to contend, to be heard and to hear is to make information human. It is a bit of an oversimplification but the need to talk to each other is where I begin. Making information human will allow the third sector to be heard and encourage governments to really listen. But how do we do that? By fostering genuine human dialogue, providing voices of integrity and building relationships, the third sector will make information human and ensure that it is heard.

Encouraging human dialogue involves honesty and seeing the big picture. In our human relationships we know that sometimes it is most challenging to be open and honest about what we want, to find all kinds of indirect ways to express our desires or wishes and then sometimes we are surprised when we do not get what we want. It has been my experience that when organizations speak to government, when they "cut through the bells and whistles" and communicate directly, honestly, openly about what they are looking for, it is easier for governments to listen. I know that sometimes it is tempting to jazz things up or package it creatively. Powerpoint anyone? (I hear that Powerpoint is now a verb, you can be "powerpointed.") The real problem is much simpler and more profound. Because of the volume of competing interests and demands on government, those organizations that speak with openness, honesty, and sincerity about what they are looking for establish quick credibility and have a better chance of being heard.

It is imperative for organizations to express their purposes honestly and directly and to do this with as much clarity as possible without oversimplifying. We tell candidates all the time that the question that they always have to answer is, why are you running? You have to answer it in one sentence. Why are you running? Why are you here? It is the same kind of message when I am working with agencies, the simple question is: What are you doing here? What is it that you are here for? And in those moments we are able to understand what we are engaged in. I think too often we get caught up in buzzwords and phrases and forget that there is no good substitute for genuine human dialogue. I know that there is discussion about the use of the term "third sector in civil society" and I think that these labels bear some further analysis. Simple human language speaks volumes. I am not sure if the term "third sector" has been useful in dealing with government.

I want to point out another key element about communication. While honesty and clarity are essential in making information human, it is important to link the information we present to the bigger picture. As you know, governments by nature are constantly forced into balancing competing demands and the need to see how decisions or movement on a certain issue will benefit the citizens, the constituents, and themselves. It is not simply arguments to appeal to government self-interest, although they in fact can be useful. But it is to say that given the volume of interest and concerns they face, governments and ministers work best when they know how a particular initiative will fit into the larger scheme of things. I see an organization succeed when they do their homework, and their research about what government is actually trying to achieve, and they then speak to that. Working and serving in the arts I have heard some people in our organization, now speaking from the third sector, use the argument that wellness improves with attending theatre or listening to music. Believe me, I use those arguments in my daily work in health policy.

I offer a final caution here. As in all relationships, when we communicate honestly and openly and when we do not, when we mislead or when we are not as direct about where we are going, there are often consequences. If governments feel the information they have been given does not hold up under scrutiny they can be somewhat reluctant to answer the phone the next time they are called. When they do answer a call, it is with a sense of hesitancy that can impede the dialogue that everyone wants. So in your quest for genuine dialogue, honesty, clarity, and sensitivity to the big picture are essential.

I believe the second key to being heard is hearing, contending in public affairs to ensure that the message is conveyed by voices that speak with integrity. The strategy of this approach is familiar to all of us who are in the field but it merits more discussion. Again, because of the volume of voices trying to get the government's ear, the integrity of representation is essential. Integrity carries the message.

In Manitoba when there is labour trouble, a problem to mediate, we have the Fox-Decent phenomenon. Some of you may know Mr. Wally Fox-Decent and in Manitoba the mention of his name ensures instant credibility in the minds of all parties to any dispute. Mr. Fox-Decent is viewed as someone of unassailable integrity and credibility. Or consider the Norrie phenomenon. Our mayor, Bill Norrie, is often used by agencies because of his integrity and credibility.

I want to share with you an experience that I have had in government since coming to office. The new government was looking for ways to balance the budget because we had arguably inherited a bit of a deficit, although the Tories did not really agree. There was a millennium fund project that would have provided about $10 million to a myriad of NGOs and government agencies to celebrate the millennium. The government decided to play "party pooper" and to divert some of the funds to more pressing priorities. One of the projects that was shelved was the history play at the Manitoba Theatre Centre with which I was quite familiar. The staff at the Centre tried to decide what to do. This was the history of Manitoba. The play had been developed, had been reviewed, the posters had been printed, and the show was ready to go. What did they do? They developed a multi-layered communication strategy employing some of the principles that we are talking about to speak to the government about the importance of this project.

As a part of this strategy they employed a playwright to send a letter. As an advocate, they chose Ian Ross, an Aboriginal playwright who had won the Governor-General's award a few years back and who was a regular contributor to CBC radio. Ian had obvious instant recognizability and credibility. I believe that one of the reasons the Theatre Centre was heard was that Ian was a person of integrity and was lending that integrity to the cause. Although we cannot always enlist Governor-General's award winners in finding that voice, someone with integrity who can speak as an advocate is an important communication strategy that makes government listen.

In politics, using nonprofit organizations to lend credibility to an issue is a strategy employed consistently. Political parties find citizens who have experienced difficulty with government services to speak about problems in the service delivery systems. I have done that many times. Charitable campaigns use popular public figures to make a case for the cause. However, I would like to suggest that these appeals are effective in direct proportion to the integrity of the person making the case. I am reminded that it was Seneca the Elder who coined the famous formula "an orator is a good person who is skilled at speaking." We can afford to forget neither side of the equation. The skill, the art of communication may spin the melody of the message but it is integrity, the goodness of which Seneca spoke, that gives that melody its harmonic depth, its resonance with governments and the public.

Of course, governments must know whom an organization represents. Governments must know who the third sector is. I have read that there is much discussion about the identity of the third sector and some have suggested that the sector does not even know itself well. The other side of the challenge is the danger that, "as intermediaries in large organizations become stakeholders in the process and final product, a gulf will be driven between those agencies and smaller and weaker ones lacking the resources or size to be heard."[2] The size

---

[2]Kathy L. Brock, "Sustaining a Relationship: Insights from Canada on Linking the Government and Third Sector," a paper presented at the Fourth International Conference of the International Society for Third Sector Research (ISTR), Dublin, 5-8 July 2000.

of organization and celebrity profiles can never substitute for the integrity of the people who deliver the message or the cause they represent. Brock warns, "It is important to preserve the unique and varied voices of the multitude of citizen organizations. The democratic character of the sector is to be preserved and fostered." And in a related vein she continues, "governments and organizations alike must be vigilant to ensure that professionalization and bureaucratization (these are long words) of the third sector do not drown out citizen voices and needs. The voluntary sector should remain a sector for civic-minded volunteers."

Governments must be attentive to these changes but only the third sector can address them in a definitive way. Integrity must cultivate skill not be subordinated to it. The third sector must always remember that the meeting is nothing without the message and the genuine needs of the people for whom the organization is advocating.

I want to make a further point about integrity. Governments are still interested in hearing groups and third sector agencies that represent just causes. Having sat in the minister's office listening to groups with multiple sclerosis arguing for new drug therapy, people with hemophilia, hepatitus C victims, and care providers, I know that their personal tragedies and concerns have an impact on government decision-making. While it is difficult to see and give in the fashion that we would like to, the very human challenge that these organizations represent are critical voices of integrity that must continue to be heard effectively.

The final point for discussion is that of building relationships. The third sector is working actively to build a good relationship with government. It is very important. By building good relations we build trust and it is because of this trust that we listen even when we disagree. It is particularly important to have a relationship of trust that will sustain both parties the next time around. It allows mistakes to happen without damaging the dialogue. This final point envelops all of the others. When we speak honestly and openly and with each other with integrity we naturally build relationships and deepen trust.

One other key element in building trust in relationships in the third sector is giving each other room to manoeuvre. In the charged dynamic of advocacy there are too many times when both sectors are put in the awkward position of "having a gun to their heads" when they need to make a critical decision. Communication strategies always need to have a face-saving component for both parties. Governments cannot afford to take embarrassment lightly and so when they are confronted with a no-win situation, an organization's bridges get burned quickly. Even when there is fundamental disagreement, there needs to be time and space to back out gracefully so the relationship can continue the next time opportunities arise. If we build solid relationships we can avoid some of these embarrassing situations. We need to build situations that are win-win for both sides.

In conclusion, I have tried to share some of my experiences in the area of communications in order to reinforce my belief in the necessity to make information human. By encouraging dialogue, speaking with voices of integrity, and building relationships we can develop stronger bridges between the third sector and government. These strategies make contenders of all of us.

Communicators at all levels commonly say that they need to be more involved. It is critical for both the third sector and governments to realize that communication is central to the process of making information human. Communicators need to be an integral part of the team. They need to truly understand our goals so that they can honour our messages and do them justice. Everyone needs to listen in order to ensure that what is said is effective and connects to the most crucial listeners. We can develop human communication strategies to advance important human endeavours. I believe that the third sector and government working together can achieve goals that we all want. Cicero said that we need laboratories to teach, to delight, to move. I hope that all our communications reflect that classic ideal and that we continue to listen to each other as we move forward into the new century with stronger relationships between government, the third sector, and the citizens that we are all privileged to serve.

DEENA WHITE
Professor of Sociology
Université de Montréal

Harnessing a Movement, Taming an Ideology: On the State and the Third Sector in Quebec

There are striking differences between Quebec and English Canada with respect to the idiom, identity, structure, and politics of the third sector. These differences persist even though both sectors have emerged within somewhat similar socio-economic and political contexts — essentially neo-liberal — which, in both cases, are causing relations between the state and the third sector to evolve and to be rethought and reworked. For a Québécois, the language of "voluntary" or "charity" organizations, so prominent in English Canada, appears old-fashioned or, more to the point, harks back to an ultra-paternalist religious tradition rather left to another era. While nonprofit grassroots organizations have a strong and increasingly influential presence in Quebec, their roots lie more in the community activism of the 1960s than in older values.

In the Anglo-Saxon tradition, the pre-eminence of the individual, of the private sphere and of civil society over the state is vivid in the public imagination. The role of the state is ideally restricted to government or management, its powers limited by common law, or the established practices of the people. Indeed, at the extreme, the state and civil society may be perceived as facing off against each other, in a contest where a highly circumscribed state and extensive individual liberty are the ideal outcome. In this context, voluntary action, seen as the altruistic behaviour of individuals, tends to be held in high moral esteem because it rises above that more coarse, self-interested action that ultimately propels society. It embraces charity and advocacy on behalf of the less fortunate, and supports culture, leisure, and other activities that are of little interest to the profit-making sector. It represents a certain collective spirit, even in the form of professional, business and consumer associations, which acts as a corrective to pure self-interest.

In Quebec, this manner of conceiving voluntary action does not capture the public imagination. Continental models of civil society, more familiar and accessible to Canada's French-speaking population, never asserted individual sovereignty in quite the same manner as in Anglo-Saxon countries. On the contrary, notions of the sovereign state, of solidarity and of para-public associations mediating between the state and the individual had greater resonance. The Church was, of course, the prototypical third-sector organization, in Quebec as elsewhere. Indeed, along with its affiliated organizations, it had full, active responsibility for promoting the welfare and culture of French-Canadian society as a whole, while minority communities in Quebec developed their own service and cultural institutions. But this is a history of organized, collective community action, rather than individual, upper-class philanthropy and middle-class charity work. Thus, in the Québécois public imagination, what stands out from this history is the collective responsibility of and for communities, not the altruistic activity of individuals. This ethos was harnessed by the Quiet Revolution of the 1960s, which swept away the power, influence, and imagery associated with the Catholic Church and replaced it with the modern leadership of the state — in Lesage's famous 1961 words: "*our* state, we cannot afford the luxury of not using it." But at the same time as the activist

Quebec state, representative of a modern Québécois community, was coming into its own, the union movement and militant citizen committees were fighting for radical institutional reform from the grassroots level. Indeed, the Quiet Revolution might rightly be seen as a double revolution, coming both from the top down and from the bottom up. It is the co-existence and the tension between these movements, one elitist and the other populist and grassroots, both sharing a "community" rhetoric, that eventually gave birth to Quebec's third sector, and continues to colour the relationship between the state and the community movement today.

The standard history of Quebec's third sector goes something like this. Church leadership of welfare and charity work at the parish level gave way in the 1960s to a new breed of local community activism, modelled after the American, syndicalist style of community action initiated by Saul Alinsky in the 1930s and adopted by community groups in the years of the War against Poverty. In Quebec, this community activism took the form of Citizen Action Committees that mushroomed in poor or working-class, urban neighbourhoods, setting up free clinics, housing cooperatives, leisure activities for youth and daycare centres for working mothers. The committees were highly politicized, inspired by the ideology of autogestion or self-management, and pressured the state to make quality health, social, and community services available to all, in a manner that would be both accessible and empowering.

In the 1970s, the modernizing state not only took many of these responsibilities onto its own shoulders, but did so in an innovative fashion inspired by the community movement. It established a network of CLSCs, or local community service centres throughout the province. These small, relatively unbureaucratic public organizations, which still exist today in about 150 communities and cover the territory of the province, conform to a government charter and receive their mandate and entire budget from the government. Initially developed in collaboration with local citizens' committees, the first CLSCs were rather chaotic affairs, and the government was quickly forced to draw a line between the desired citizen *participation,* and citizen *control,* which often led to idiosyncratic programs and practices, at odds with the CLSC mandate. The history of tension between citizen committees and the CLSCs is legend in the Quebec community movement and serves to illustrate the tendency of the state to appropriate grassroots action and transform it to meet government-defined objectives.

The establishment of the CLSC eventually led the community movement to split. Some aspects of community action were taken over by professional community organizers, drawn into the CLSCs and rapidly "tamed," as these organizations became increasingly institutionalized over the years. The remaining leaders of the movement became more radically politicized, to the extent that eventually they lost touch with the grassroots community entirely. After a strident start, autonomous community action became nearly invisible in Quebec for almost a decade, essentially eclipsed by the CLSCs.

Community groups finally began a quiet resurgence in the 1980s, responding to new needs at the community level, exacerbated by the recession and by draconian cuts to health and social services in the public sector. Alternative mental health resources were among the first of these service-oriented organizations to appear, in response to those needs created by deinstitutionalization. Women's shelters, daycare centres, and youth centres also appeared, all filling in where needs were not being met by the CLSCs. Funding for these new community groups was exceedingly difficult to come by and many had an erratic and short lifespan. However, they were supported by their shared identity as members of an alternative community movement, struggling against the inadequate, bureaucratized, state-sponsored version of community services. They organized themselves into local and regional roundtables and provincial associations to demand recognition and support from the government in order to deal with the growing un-met needs in their communities.

Despite the increasing political organization of the third sector, to share information and defend its autonomy, many groups were drawn into partnerships with para-public organizations such as hospitals and social service centres and even government departments. In a few cases, they became little more than subcontracted service providers. In 1991, legislation to reform the health and social services system officially included community organizations in its definition of its network of establishments, previously consisting only of para-public entities such as hospitals and CLSCs. Funding from the Ministry of Health and Social Services increased exponentially as community groups were contracted to provide services such as home care, which would be too expensive to implement in the professionalized, unionized CLSCs. Also, new "workfare" programs funded by the Ministry of Income Security became an important source of badly needed labour for community service groups, and contributed to the rapid growth of the third sector during the 1990s. Ideologically, the community movement opposed funding that used them to implement government-defined programs, or compelled welfare recipients to work in their organizations for little more than their basic welfare cheque, without the social status of regular workers. But compromises were made to gain the funding necessary to meet community needs, while at the same time, the provincial associations and regional tables of third sector organizations challenged the

government's view of partnership. State-third sector relations during this period came to be characterized by observers in such terms as "cooperative conflict," "contradictory participation," and "critical cooperation."[3]

The introduction into Quebec culture, during the 1990s, of the concept of
the "social economy," is often seen as another step in this same history of the
appropriation of grassroots movements by the state. If the idea of the social
economy — or the development of a socially useful third sector as a source of
employment — initially inspired community economic development groups,
this idea, too, was quickly pounced upon by certain government actors as a
brilliant way to respond to the paradox that social needs remain unmet while
thousands of Quebecers, able to respond to these needs, seek work. As we
shall see, the social economy was transformed in the hands of the state, as
well.

But there is another side to the story of state-third sector relations in Quebec that is less often told. What is, from one perspective, "appropriation" of
the community movement by the state may, from another perspective, be seen
as the community movement's influence on the state. For example, the establishment of the para-public CLSC network in the 1970s may have had the per-
verse effect of temporarily eclipsing autonomous community action at the grassroots level, but regardless, the CLSCs themselves learned a great deal from
community action. Aside from providing primary health and social services
and implementing province-wide prevention programs, they have consistently
reached out to communities and helped them to organize to meet their own
particular needs, as far as possible. Many of the community organizations of
the 1980s were either born with help from CLSC community organizers or
were supported by them, if not financially then through technical help and
advice. In other words, the influence of the early citizens' committees on

---

[3]The Quebec literature on this subject is prolific. For example, P. Maclouf, "Les
restructurations économiques et l'ancrage territorial de la crise de l'État-
providence," *Revue internationale d'action communautaire* 13, 53(1985); J. Panet-
Raymond, "Community Groups in Quebec: From Radical Action to Voluntarism for
the State?" *Commununity Development Journal* 22, 4(1997):281-86; D. White, "La
gestion communautaire de l'exclusion," *Lien social et Politiques – Revue
internationale d'action communautaire* 32(1994):37-51; D. White, "Contradictory
Participation: Reflections on Community Action in Quebec," in *Community Organizing: Canadian Experiences*, ed. B. Wharf and M. Clague (Oxford: Oxford
University Press, 1997).

government intervention at the community level has been significant and long-lasting. This strong, bottom-up influence was equally evident in the impact of the community movement on, for example, the transformation of mental health services in Quebec, community economic development and the establishment of Quebec's policy of universal, $5-a-day daycare.

The reciprocal relations and tensions between the state and the community sector are best illustrated by events that have occurred since 1995. In order to better support its policy of partnership with the community sector, the government announced, in April 1995, the creation of a Secretariat for Autonomous Community Action, to be attached directly to the Executive Council. Two months later, to confirm the community movement's principal objective to fight for social justice, and to challenge any new government strategy to appropriate popular power for its own ends, a coalition of women's groups, poverty organizations, and students descended on the National Assembly in Quebec City for the March for Bread and Roses. One year later, at a provincial socio-economic summit held in 1996, the community sector was offered a seat along-side government, business, and union sectors as one of the province's influential "partners." While this and other more recent summits are best character-ized as orchestrated exercises in consensus-building by the Quebec govern-ment, they nonetheless have a real, if limited impact on politics. At the 1996 summit, the premier of Quebec gained the consensus he sought on a zero-deficit policy, but the community contingent was also able to pressure the state, business, and union sectors to agree to create an Anti-Poverty Fund to be in-vested in job-creation programs for the poor. The fund and the summit in gen-eral proved to be the impetus for the promotion of Quebec's social economy.

It is perhaps useful at this point to distinguish between three different forms of reference used to refer to various aspects of the community movement that have emerged in Quebec. All nonprofit organizations are generally referred to as "community groups," but the "community movement" is understood to re-fer to that core of ideologically alternative, politicized community groups, and their representative roundtables and associations, that play the leadership role in state-third sector relations in the province. Recently, this vanguard has adopted the term "autonomous community action" to refer to all community groups that claim to share its ultimate mission or general ideology, which will be outlined further on. As for the "social economy," it emerged as an integral part of the community movement but representing a particular *vision* of that movement: one that recognizes not only the important social contribution of the third sector but also its significant economic potential in the post-Fordist context of high unemployment rates and a shrinking public sector.

The ideological influence of the community movement on the Quebec state is evident in state discourse. Take, for example, the very name of the secretariat that the government created in 1995 to support and develop the third sector in partnership with the state: The Secretariat for Autonomous Community Action. With the sector formally defined in terms of *action* rather than type of organization, the emphasis is less on services and structures than on social engagement. "Community action" tends to be distinguished from both "community organizing" and "community planning," as more grassroots-led and concerned with fundamental social change. Even in official government descriptions of the sector, it is explicitly stated that the struggle against impoverishment and social exclusion constitutes the core concern around which both advocacy and service organizations actively build their solidarity as a movement in Quebec. But the gap between government discourse and policy is as wide here as in any other domain, and the movement itself is not as unified as one might be led to imagine.

The official mandate of the Secretariat for Autonomous Community Action includes facilitating community groups' access to government resources; advising the government on how best to support community action; and fostering a better understanding of the sector.[4] It also administers the Fund for Autonomous Community Action through which it provides direct support to organizations. The Fund for Autonomous Community Action is generated by the state lotteries: 5 percent of the annual net take of state casinos goes into the fund, which amounted, in 1998–99, to a little over $12.5 million. This was distributed to some 660 organizations that year, some new, some not, for an average grant of just under $20,000 each.

This fund is designed to meet several objectives. It is intended, first, to provide support for civil rights groups whose primary activity is the defence of the social and political rights of the disenfranchised, be they welfare recipients, the mentally ill, the handicapped, ethnic minorities, or others. Second, it is intended to support services to families, youth, the elderly, the poor, and other vulnerable populations, with a view to "promoting greater social justice," especially for the worst off in society. Everything from food banks and collective kitchens to alternative mental health resources and needle exchanges

---

[4]The factual information presented here on the mandate and activities of the secretariat is drawn principally from its annual report for 1998–99, available on the Internet at <http://saca.gouv.qc.ca/>.

may receive funding. Third, the money is intended to build the capacity of the sector itself. This usually means contributing to specific projects such as colloquia or special events sponsored by regional roundtables or provincial associations, as well as to Community Development Corporations, which work to promote community action and values at the local level. Women's roundtables are also listed as eligible for financing by the secretariat, for their role not only in advocacy and popular education, but also in defending and promoting women's interests and rights. All in all, it is clear that a major element of the secretariat's mandate is to promote capacity-building and advocacy, and in fact a good 40 percent of its fund goes toward those types of activities as opposed to services.

In April 2000, as part of its mandate, the secretariat published a consultation document proposing the terms of a government policy with respect to the sector.[5] At the outset, the proposal explicitly recognized that "community action is a genuine social movement in its own right, whose components are widely diverse and ever-shifting." Furthermore, it recognized the following five principles of autonomous community action, as elaborated by the advisory council to the secretariat, made up of representatives of the movement:

- The goal of autonomous community action is social development and transformation, as well as the creation of opportunities for democratic action and the expression of citizenship in every sphere of civil society. It works toward the emergence of a more humane society, open to the world and its diversity, and toward improving quality of life through the struggle against poverty, discrimination, and exclusion.
- Community action is born of the initiatives of community members and engages them, working to build up networks and mutual aid practices within the community.
- It is holistic and empowering in its orientation.
- It achieves its objectives through alternative, innovative practices, advocacy, popular education, and rapid response to changing social conditions.

---

[5]Secrétariat à l'action communautaire autonome du Quebec (2000), *Le milieu communautaire: un acteur essentiel au développement du Quebec. Proposition de politique* (Quebec: Ministère de la solidarité sociale). Excerpts are the author's translation.

- Its autonomy is primordial, that is, the real possibility for organizations to determine their mission, orientations, priorities and practices, and to evaluate themselves and determine their own internal rules and norms.

The policy would apply to all nonprofit organizations with a social mission that subscribe to the five principles of community action mentioned above, that are anchored in their community (i.e., obtain some resources from the community itself, for example, in the form of volunteers or donations in money or in kind), and that are associative and democratic in their internal organization.

Having subscribed to a highly ideological definition of autonomous community action, the Quebec government's proposed terms of partnership were rather less radical. First, it would streamline the dealings between community groups and the government by setting up a basic set of norms to be applied by all government departments, with slight adaptations to take the particular circumstances of each into account. Second, any government department working in partnership with community groups would be required to offer "accreditation" to the organizations that it finances, thus acknowledging those organizations that "belong" to its sector of activity. Third, the policy proposes that departments offer three-year core funding grants to accredited organizations. Thus, all departments must agree to support not only the specific services that they would like to see implemented, but also the general operating and payroll costs of the organization, the costs of participating in meetings, training employees, educating the public, and supporting volunteers, as well as the costs related to advocacy and sectoral capacity-building. In return, community organizations would agree to obtain community input in some form, to keep transparent accounts and report yearly to the department in question, and to be evaluated, using methods acceptable to them.

Overall, the proposal appeared to be narrowly concerned with regulating relations between community organizations and state departments. Other provisions expressed government support for access to better employee benefits in the third sector, as well as for providing capital and training. But the main objectives appeared to be administrative: to ensure that government support for the community sector is fairly distributed and uniformly regulated among the many departments that turn to the third sector in the context of meeting their objectives. For community organizations, it would facilitate access to reliable, basic funding for those recognized as "belonging" to one government department or another, funding that goes well beyond payment for contracted services.

In April 2000, the policy proposal was distributed throughout the province for consultation purposes. By the deadline of 31 July, more than 600 briefs from a wide variety of organizations and associations had been received by the secretariat. Gérald Larose, a former union leader and popular figure in Quebec, led the consultation. He reviewed the briefs and held 29 meetings across the province in which more than 2,000 people participated. His report, published on 6 November 2000, suggested that the policy proposal missed the mark.[6] The community movement expected it would focus on supporting and promoting autonomous community action, but instead it appeared to concentrate mainly on the manner in which community groups could be helped to contribute to government objectives and priorities. There were three types of reactions from community activists: outright rejection of partnership with the state; acceptance of some sort of partnership in principle but highly critical of the form suggested in the policy; and finally, acceptance of partnerships in some circumstances, but insistence that these represent only one aspect of the relations between community groups and the state. Those relations also include confrontation and conflict, a fact that some argued needed to be acknowledged in the policy.

The consultation process highlighted an important contradiction in the policy proposal and also allowed certain divisions within the community sector itself to rise to the surface. Not all community groups in Quebec are part of the community movement after all, or at least, not all are involved in *autonomous* community action as this is defined in the policy proposal. Some identify themselves simply as community organizations providing services that complement or supplement those offered in the public sector, and whether they do so in an alternative, empowering or democratic fashion is not significant for their self-definition. They are not necessarily seeking to promote social justice on a broad scale. For those who already have a recognized status within various government departments, the policy proposal may indeed have represented a significant improvement in their relations with the state. The community movement, however, had invested considerable political energy in selling the concept of *autonomous* community *action*, convincing the government to recognize its

---

[6]G. Larose, *Propostion de Politique de soutien et de reconnaissance de l'action communautaire: Le milieu communautaire, un acteur essentiel au développement du Quebec. Rapport de la consultation publique* (Quebec: Ministère de la solidarité sociale, 2000).

role and importance in the naming of the secretariat and in the definition of the role and place of the community movement in the policy proposal. Although the government proposal used the term "autonomous community action," and defined it in a manner acceptable to the movement, it then went on to discuss government relations with groups providing *complementary* services in various government domains.

The framework suggested in the policy proposal, some believed, would clearly subvert autonomous community action, in which service provision, if carried out in a particular manner, is but one of the means used to work toward broader social objectives of social justice and empowerment. Any group that would become associated with, and dependent upon, a particular government department using standardized government norms for its dealings with the third sector, could hardly expect to determine its own mission, orientations, priorities, practices, and internal rules and norms. The risk of becoming accountable to the department, in order to maintain funding status, would surely interfere with an organization's obligation to be accountable first and foremost to its constituency. Furthermore, associating with a single government department would necessarily force these groups into a sectoral mould that would go against their holistic approach to social problems and issues. Taking these inconsistencies into account, the recommendations made to government on the basis of the consultation process highlighted the distinction between nonprofit or community service groups *in general*, and "autonomous community action." They suggest ways in which both can be recognized and accommodated in accordance with their particular, but different roles in society.[7]

While this official policy addresses community action, the third sector in Quebec is also thought of in terms of the social economy. The concept is based on the premise that, if public provision of services is bureaucratic, expensive, insensitive to diversity and change, and generally inefficient, then autonomous, nonprofit or cooperative, community-based service provision may be the

---

[7]In June 2001, the Cabinet adopted a final, official policy, revised in light of the consultation results. Significantly more attention is paid to the values and principles of autonomous community action throughout the policy, and the link between community organizations and individual government departments has been loosened, allowing for considerably more flexibility, including funding from more than one source. The final policy was published too late to be fully analyzed for this paper.

answer — provided these organizations are adequately supported. More importantly, though, the development of this new service sector would expand the labour market, providing jobs in socially useful areas that are underserved. Home care and daycare, environmental protection and recycling, labour force integration programs for the disabled or other hard-to-place people and so on, are all currently in great demand. But they are either unavailable or inaccessible through the private market, or are inadequately addressed in the public sector. The expansion of the social economy would increase employment in such areas, in not-for-profit enterprises with a strong social mission.

This view of the social economy has been adopted by the *Chantier de l'économie sociale* (Social Economy Worksite), a nonprofit organization created and funded in the wake of the socio-economic summit of 1996. Made up of representatives of the community and cooperative movements, women's groups, and local development, cultural, and environmental groups, its mission is to promote the development of the social economy, represent it to government bodies, mobilize the private sector to support it, and collaborate with both the public and private sectors in their dealings with the social economy. Eventually, the *Chantier* might be called upon to form a secretariat similar to that for autonomous community action. In the meantime, it promotes the view that social economy enterprises must generate good, permanent jobs and provide a socially just and empowering working environment if ever they are to play their intended role in society.

However, the Quebec model of the social economy has come to diverge somewhat from this ideal. The development of the social economy here has instead taken an essentially *entrepreneurial* approach. Although not-for-profit or cooperative in form, and involved in the production of socially useful goods and services, social economy organizations in Quebec are expected to be financially viable enterprises, able to compete in the marketplace with private enterprises. While the government may help to set them up and may compensate for aspects of these organizations that make them less competitive than traditional enterprises (e.g., the nature of their workforce, clientele, product or service offered), they are required to become self-sufficient within three years.

The emphasis that is today placed on self-sufficiency and competitiveness relates back to the origins of the Anti-Poverty Fund that, since 1997, is supposed to finance much of the social economy. The Anti-Poverty Fund was created by the business and labour sectors, who did not want their voluntary contributions to go into "social" services for the poor, nor into the development of a parallel economy, where some enterprises would benefit from generous grants while being sheltered from the risks of doing business in a competitive market.

It was therefore determined that the Anti-Poverty Fund would only finance social economy enterprises with business plans that met the expectation of rapid self-sufficiency. This has had a tremendous impact on the way in which the social economy has recently developed in Quebec.

The Anti-Poverty Fund generated about $160 million over its first three years, and was renewed for another three years in 1999, at another summit where the same partners were present.[8] Most of the money spent has gone toward salaries for people employed in the social economy. In the first three years, 161 new social economy enterprises were created, generating 7,992 jobs. The new jobs were developed in several key areas. For example, hundreds of early childhood centres have been set up since 1997, all in the nonprofit sector, to meet the needs of the Quebec child-care policy. Likewise, in the area of home help, hundreds of organizations have come into being to meet the needs of the health system reform begun in 1995, known as the *virage ambulatoire,* which reduces hospital use by maintaining and treating people in the community and in their homes. Adapting workplaces for people with disabilities was formerly financed in large part by the OPHQ (Office des personnes handicapées du Quebec) but this is now done through the social economy, as are many other labour market reintegration services which help the hard-to-employ re-enter the labour force. Halfway houses for youth in child-protection services are also being set up in the social economy.

In other words, a large number of government departments find the social economy a preferable way of delivering new services that would not have existed 20 or 30 years ago, or if they had, would have been offered as public services — at least in Quebec. The Ministries of Education, Health and Social Services, Justice, Regional Development, Family and Children, and others all deal with social economy enterprises. The question is, how are these relations different from those between government departments and autonomous community action groups, or straight nonprofit organizations offering complementary services, often in these same areas? Social economy enterprises — like all community organizations — are ideally expected to use democratic decision-making processes, and to foster collective participation and responsibility. Moreover, given the ideological and theoretical underpinnings

---

[8]The factual information and quotations presented in this section were obtained from the Quebec government's social economy Web site, *Oser l'économie sociale,* at <http://www.cex.gouv.qc.ca/economiesociale>.

of the social economy, it should be an active promoter of and contributor to a more just society.

Indeed, some see the social economy as another stage or phase in the community movement, whose ultimate objective is broad, fundamental social change. Thus, in the journal *Recto-Verso,* an activist made the following observation: "Community groups, which have for 30 years waved their placards in all directions, are today entering the perilous world of business, and trying to contaminate the economy with the social values they hold dear." To which the president of the Banque Nationale, an enthusiastic supporter of the social economy, remarked: "Don't you worry, it won't contaminate a thing! Social economy enterprises will very quickly develop a business mentality, or they will fail."[9] In 1999, the Executive Council stated that

> It is extremely important to keep in perspective that the government's support for the community movement takes two separate directions: on the one hand, a financial contribution to community organizations; on the other hand, a desire to promote and support the emergence and development of social economy enterprises in certain solvent sectors of activity.[10]

What exactly is the difference between the social economy and community organizations that this government statement refers to? Why is it extremely important to keep them separate? For in some cases, it might appear that an organization may be defined as either one or the other. A nonprofit agency whose mission is to help integrate the disabled into the labour market, for example, would be considered a community organization if it offered training, job placement or support services; it would be a social economy enterprise if its principal mission was to actually employ the disabled. There are, of course, a number of agencies that do both. Either way, we might wonder at the insistence that the two types of organizations be kept distinct.

Social economy funds are destined mainly for salaries and aim to support as many new employees as possible, while community action groups tend to be

---

[9]"Économie sociale: Ces entreprises qui veulent changer le monde," *Recto-Verso* 275 (1998):3.

[10]Ministère du Conseil exécutif, *Position gouvernmentale sur la tarification dans les entreprises de l'économie sociale*, Secrétariat du Sommet sur l'économie et l'emploi, 3 février 1999 et révisé le 9 juin 1999. At <www.cex.gouv.qc.ca/economiesociale/html/Tarification.html> (Author's translation).

small, with relatively few employees, and ostensibly require less to keep them going. But it is not the use to which grants might be put that is really significant, nor the needs of the organization. It is rather the source of those funds that accounts for the distinction between these two kinds of third sector organizations. Social economy enterprises are mainly (though not solely) supported by business and unions, through the Anti-Poverty Fund, and are ultimately expected to fend for themselves. Community organizations are different in that their entire mission is *social* rather than "socio-economic." Once an organization is involved in hiring people to produce goods and services that will be sold on the market, it is deemed to have an economic mission, even if its *raison d'être* is clearly not profit maximization. Therefore, there is a whole framework of norms and relations into which a social economy enterprise must fit, especially if it is to be supported by business and labour through the Anti-Poverty Fund.

Pressure for maintaining the distinction thus comes from two interested parties outside government: business and unions. Both are concerned that the Anti-Poverty Fund, to which they voluntarily agreed to contribute, be used strictly for job creation and not for social services nor for development of a parallel economy. But the community movement is *also* wary of being too closely associated with the social economy, with its apparent emphasis on the economic rather than the social aspects of its mission. From its perspective, concern for production, job creation, and revenue often obscures the "ultimate" objectives of participation, empowerment, education, advocacy, and social justice.

The discomfort of the community movement with recent trends in the social economy also reflects a very old ideological split in the movement. On the one hand, there have always been those organizations whose struggle is based on improving community ties, living conditions and social justice for the poor. On the other hand, there have been those inspired by the ideology of autogestion and the belief that participation in the labour force is, in the last instance, most important; without good jobs, the poor will always be poor. These views certainly do not oppose each other, but highlighting the distinction between community groups and social economy groups has brought this dormant schism closer to the surface.

Through all of this, the government's strategies for managing its relations with the various sorts of organizations are really quite consistent. In all cases, the aim is to encourage a wide variety of government departments to enter into stable and respectful partnerships with nongovernmental organizations, to help respond to the growing and diversifying imperatives of their sector, be those social or economic. As for the conditions placed on social economy enterprises by the contributors to the Anti-Poverty Fund, these are not yet written in stone. Far fewer enterprises than anticipated have been created through the Anti-Poverty Fund. Indeed, many local development councils are having great difficulty spending their social economy budgets. This is because few social economy enterprises, if any, can develop a business plan that both responds to the social needs that they want to address and promises market viability within three years. Besides, any organization — private or not-for-profit — still has access to salary subsidies through the traditional welfare-to-work programs of the Ministry of Social Solidarity, whether or not it adheres to the formal conditions for access to the Anti-Poverty Fund.[11]

Rather than place an emphasis on the distinction between the social economy and the community movement, it may be more instructive to take a closer look at what they have in common. The social economy, the Anti-Poverty Fund that finances its development and the Secretariat of Autonomous Community Action all fall under the purview of a single department, the Ministry of Social Solidarity and Employment. The broad sector for which this ministry is responsible is significant: this is the department responsible for social assistance and welfare-to-work programs, for the "war against poverty." The clientele of this ministry is the same marginalized population that is typically addressed by both the community movement and the social economy, as service users, employees, or volunteers. Indeed, we are looking at a multi-faceted third sector that is itself, in a sense, ensconced in a zone of exclusion.

Since the 1970s, it has been the Ministry of Health and Social Services that has had the most prominent relations with the community sector, and even the social economy was, at first, a pet project promoted from within that department. That department is now only one of many dealing with the third sector, even though its contributions still outstrip most others. And the department that now has the mandate to orchestrate relations with the sector as a whole —

---

[11]An auditor general's report suggested that it is in fact very difficult to know exactly where the money from the Anti-Poverty Fund goes, and that much of it may have been spent to cover deficits associated with welfare-to-work programs. This could occur since salary subsidies financed by the fund and those financed by the government within its welfare-to-work policy, are both managed by the same department. Vérificateur générale du Quebec, *Rapport à l'Assemblée nationale pour l'année 1998-99* (Quebec: Publications du Quebec, 1999), vol. 1, ch. 2.

the Ministry of Social Solidarity and Employment — is one with a very different culture. It is highly centralized, with no experience in working with the community movement, and has historically been concerned only with applying the welfare law and clearing the welfare rolls through labour force integration programs. It is used to dealing with the most marginal and stigmatized population within the province, in a relationship of control more than in a helping relationship. That both community action and the social economy fall within its purview suggests that the government may still be taking a particularly instrumental view of the sector, with little understanding of its five defining characteristics mentioned earlier. Is the third sector to become the public service sector for the destitute?

Perhaps not, as long as it continues to use its political savvy to collectively contest government strategies that would rob it of its historical and evolving identity. The impression outside Quebec is that the third sector there is more politically sophisticated than in many other jurisdictions, and that state-third sector relations have achieved a level as yet unknown elsewhere in the country. This might actually be a fairly accurate impression. The third sector and the state have indeed been politically engaged with each other since the 1960s. Governments of all stripes have made important efforts — from CLSCs to summits — to harness the community movement to the objectives of the state, but have found that it has not been easy to tame the grassroots, populist ideology that continues to drive it. There are now signs that the market economy may also be trying to absorb the social economy. In the meantime, internal divisions within the third sector are being laid out for public discussion. We now have autonomous community action, community organizations, and social economy enterprises, each requiring different treatment and wanting to be recognized for what they are and for their particular roles in society. This can only be a good thing, for highlighting the diversity within the sector is likely to highlight as well the common ground between these different dimensions of the community movement.

On the other hand, this tension has made it clear that the community movement or sector has its own corporate interests, just as the business, labour, and public sectors do. Harmonious relations with the state would not be in its interests; the "cooperative conflict" that it has perfected over four decades may be far more suited, and in fact far more similar, to the relations that exist between the business and labour sectors and the state. It remains to be seen whether the Quebec government has learned to live with this kind of relationship as well, or whether it will be given a choice. The community movement has shown no signs of dissipating in Quebec; in fact, if the leadership role it played in the International March of Women in October 2000 is of any significance, it may be that the movement is growing and maturing.

Finally, the Quebec case suggests that a change in the institutional relations between the state and the third sector may ultimately involve the other sectors as well. The more the third sector is drawn into institutional relations with the state, the more the interests of business, labour, and the public sector impinge on that relationship and on the third sector itself. However, in Quebec, at least, there is some hope and even a suggestion that the third sector is also a social actor that can impinge on the others. However limited its power may be, the community movement has nonetheless lent its idiom to the Quebec state, structured the provision of certain public services such as daycare and mental health services, encouraged the labour movement to take up its cause and "forced" the economic sector to admit some responsibility for the jobless. Notably, this grassroots influence, as circumscribed as it may be, has developed within a state-centred and pseudo-corporatist political culture, particular to Quebec. Can it emerge as well in the more civil-society-centred, common-law cultures of the rest of Canada?

HAL GEREIN
Deputy Minister
Community Development, Cooperatives and Volunteers
British Columbia

Working with the Third Sector

Although we on Canada's west coast, or as cartoonists would have it "the left coast," have a unique experience and our own perspective in terms of the provincial government's relationship with the sector, we have much to learn and are in the early stages of what I would call a developing relationship. To describe this relationship, I will discuss a little about the following: the sector in British Columbia and some of its characteristics; the history of the province's relationship with elements of the sector; the creation of a Cabinet portfolio to recognize the importance of the sector; working with the sector and government's explicit policy on program objectives; and some of the challenges to this developing relationship.

Broadly, we speak of the three pillars of economic organization in western democracies: the market or the business sector, the public sector, and the not-for-profit or third sector. BC's third sector is made up of some 21,853 societies and 551 cooperatives in addition to the federally registered nonprofits and provincial quasi-public institutions with charitable status. The truth is that very little is known about these 22,000 organizations. We have not categorized them or studied their inputs or their outputs. The 1997 National Survey on Volunteering, Giving and Participating provided the following characteristics of BC's population: of our population aged 15 and over, 73 percent were donors; one million British Columbians volunteered their time, a rate of 32 percent; and 54 percent participated in civic activities through voluntary associations. These characteristics are, in fact, not uncharacteristic of the rest of the nation. This brief profile illustrates the significance of the sector and volunteerism to the daily lives of British Columbians, and hence, is of interest to governments who, as we know, tax, spend, regulate, and redistribute income.

Governments at all levels have had a long-standing and formal relationship with the market sector. These are legal relationships treating businesses as persons, with tax and government program relationships that recognize that it is the market sector's importance to the economy. Similarly, we have had years of experience with intergovernmental relations, with defined law and a constitution with a division of powers and responsibilities to guide us. Yet, when it comes to the third sector, the third pillar, that broadly defined grouping of not-for-profits and activities dedicated to being the "glue that binds society together," we wonder if it is appropriate to have a designated ministry or lead organizations that would be responsive to it. What took us so long?

Generalizing a great deal, I would describe British Columbia's historical relationship with the sector up to the past 20 years or so as one of mutual benefit and benign neglect. In the 1990s, however, the province determined that its relationships with the sector had resulted in a proliferation of social service organizations leading to unnecessary competition and high administrative costs. The ministries began what was dubbed "a contract review process" to streamline their service relationships with the sector. Larger not-for-profits and longer term contracts emerged. Public service unions moved to unionize many of the sector's organizations contributing to the ongoing and complex issues of pay equity and paid versus unpaid work. Jeremy Rifkin in his book, *The End of Work* forecasts that "the government is likely to play a far different role in the emerging high-tech era, one far less tied to the interests of the commercial economy and more aligned with the interests of the social economy. Forging a new partnership between the government and third sector to rebuild a social economy could help restore civic life in every nation."[12]

The province and its constituents recognize the sector as an essential component in the overall social and economic health of the province. It was in April 1998 that BC named the first-ever minister with responsibility for and to the voluntary sector. This responsibility was consolidated with other functions in July 1999 in a new Ministry of Community Development, Cooperatives and Volunteers. The ministry's mission is to promote, support, and invest in community efforts that encourage all British Columbians to build and maintain healthy, self-reliant communities reflecting the goals, aspirations, and participation of their citizens. Our mission is currently carried out through five centres of activity and programming: community development; transition and adjustment services for communities suffering from the economic trauma of a major mill closure or plant closures; community enterprise that focuses on economic diversification; cooperatives and volunteers who focus on the building of a social economy and the third sector as elements of community; and, of course, intergovernmental relations, research, and strategic initiatives. We are also responsible for the provincial leadership of the Vancouver agreement, a five-year, local-provincial-federal partnership aimed at the recovery and revitalization of the city's most impoverished and marginalized areas.

In essence, our work is to forge what Rifkin would refer to as new partnerships to contribute to the building of civil life. The ministry is committed to carrying out its mission using a community development approach. That is, carrying out its work in such a manner as to contribute to the capacity of the community to know itself, to gain those resources and authorities appropriate to the management of its own future and to undertake action to enhance its social, economic, and environmental conditions. What this has meant to our ministry is that our programs and services would be built in partnership with the sector.

In January 1999, the province released a draft voluntary sector strategy and in December 1999 reported its findings. Based on its consultation work, the ministry developed four principles to guide its relationship with the sector:

- government, business, labour and the voluntary sector have a role to play building community and should work together;

---

[12]Jeremy Rifkin, *The End of Work: The Decline of the Global Labour Force and the Dawn of the Post-Market Era* (New York: G.P. Putnam's Sons, 1995), p. 250.

- the capacity and potential of the voluntary sector and its contribution to the community should be recognized and promoted;
- the autonomy, diversity and capacity of the sector should be respected; and
- the voluntary sector should be a partner at the public policy table.

These principles responded to three key messages we heard in our consultations. The voluntary sector organizations were pleased to have a minister to speak to their interests at the Cabinet table; voluntary sector organizations were pleased to receive government recognition; and voluntary sector organizations made it very clear that the minister was not its representative.

The ministry further conferred with the sector agencies which I refer to as the "sector forum" to discuss the offering of government program resources in order to begin to address the mutuality of program objectives. These objectives were: (i) to recognize and promote volunteerism and the work of the voluntary sector; (ii) to enhance the capacity of the sector; (iii) to advance the relationship between the sector and government and promote partnerships with other sectors; and (iv) to enable voluntary organizations to promote the development of creative solutions to community issues.

Following this preliminary consultation, a first offering of program resources under InVOLve BC was made. Out of over 400 proposals requesting some $14 million in support, only 119 projects, along with several innovation projects, could be funded. A funded proposal included, for example, a project by the Western Association of Directors of Volunteers to develop consistent benchmarks, standards of practice and outcome measures for volunteer management. We believe that these innovation projects can contribute to the "slack capacity" that organizations and the sector need to change themselves, to increase their interconnectedness, and to create essential coalitions as the sector redefines itself to meet the changing needs of the communities it serves. This year the ministry reported back to the sector forum reviewing its funding criteria, its process, and its decisions. The ministry has made significant efforts to maintain a transparent process, advancing with the sector mutual priorities for this fiscal year, and gaining the forum's endorsement and support.

Coming back, more specifically, to the voluntary sector and government's relationship with it, we are advancing a number of initiatives. We are working with other provincial and territorial governments to share information on sector programs and to determine and build on best practices. In March 2000, the ministry hosted the first provincial-territorial meeting of senior officials having responsibility for community development and the voluntary sector. British

Columbia is one of five or six provinces with a minister responsible for government relations with the sector. While our government is forward looking with its InVOLveBC program, and possibly with our philosophical orientation it is not as progressive as Quebec in terms of institutional change, making the sector a concern of every ministry of government. We are making efforts to do so. When it came to gaming regulation and revenue distribution we did not have a Wild Rose or Trillium foundation. And we learned that the federal announcement of nearly $100 million as a voluntary sector initiative captured our attention and gave rise to various responses across jurisdictions.

BC's sector forum is also pursuing a voluntary sector accord for British Columbia as a special International Year of Volunteers (2001) project. This would be an agreement that would provide a formal framework for the relationship between government and the voluntary sector. It should not be a surprise to anyone in terms of its content. Prime Minister Tony Blair has called the English compact, "a document of both practical and symbolic importance." The province agrees that an accord could be so for us as well, and it could be our legacy for the future. With Volunteer BC's leadership, we are working with a special International Year of Volunteers committee to help groups across the province plan activities and events for the year of celebration. The sector forum has also agreed that a BC volunteer screening initiative is a provincial priority. Volunteer BC, Sport BC, and the Red Cross are lead sector organizations along with the government's attorney general. We are also looking at how legislation and policies affect voluntary organizations and their interactions with the community, the three levels of government, and the private sector; and this includes investigating liability issues for directors and volunteers.

The sector in British Columbia has many reservations about government: a feeling that government has downloaded its responsibility in many regards and when doing so has not attached cash, and that the ministry may not be around for long. The sector is leery about what Paddy Bowen would call "drive-by funding" — funding that is not core or that is perceived as a temporary investment to curry political favour. Clearly, trust is a key element to any relationship and is one that government can only build through complete transparency in its objectives, in its organization, and in its financial partnerships.

Any successful relationship also appreciates the interdependencies of today's complex society. Clearly, from our regional perspective, the jurisdictional landscape affecting the sector across Canada is not level and, of course, must respect the jurisdiction of each: of Canada, of the provinces, and of local government structures. We wish only to have multilateral dialogue with the objectives of complementarity and synergy of effort and of harmonization of public policy as might affect the sector. Challenges and opportunities emerged in recognizing these interdependencies and linkages. Each province in this country has its own unique condition with respect to the voluntary sector. These conditions must be recognized and respected as we recognize and respect the diversity and the very essence of the sector as it reflects the aspirations and needs of the communities and our citizens.

The ministry's principal objective then in relating to the third sector is one of facilitating community development as a process associated with building and maintaining healthy and sustainable communities. We know that community development cannot be pursued from the outside. The actions of volunteers and not-for-profit organizations, their leadership and coalition-building are necessary ingredients to continuing to mobilize the participation of people of all ages and cultures and community efforts to a healthy civil society.

The voluntary sector has always been and must continue to be a part of that development in partnership with business and government. However, the sector's independence, hence its passion, compassion, and responsiveness to local issues and needs must be jealously guarded. As the government moves to relate to it, it is important that the sector not become overinstitutionalized. This would sap those very qualities of democracy, social cohesion, and humanity that are its strength and allure.

SELECTED COMMENTS FROM THE DISCUSSION

PAUL PROSS
Dalhousie University

I was struck by the complexity of arrangements within the Privy Council Office of the federal government for overseeing the arrangements of the Voluntary Sector Initiative. These presentations have focused on a significant problem in government involvement with the third sector. Where do you locate the point of interaction within government? Where do you locate the responsibility within government for connecting with the third sector? BC has established an agency with responsibility across the board which seems like a good idea and may be effective in some ways but in other ways struck me like the former federal agency DREE, a horizontal agency that had a lot of difficulty interacting over time with deliverers of services and suppliers of funds. Manitoba is talking about a particular agency addressing groups within the purview of that agency. In Quebec, there is an agency that is looking at groups but is really based within a ministry oriented to social services, thus excluding a number of groups. To bring the federal government in here, the central agencies are looking after these organizations, but the life span of such arrangements is generally short. There are four different models. What are the relative advantages and disadvantages of these approaches?

TERRY GOERTZEN

In Manitoba, the secretariat is fairly inclusive of a broad range of groups throughout the province. It is a real strength. However, with respect to the idea of engagement through one agency, it is important that groups retain their sense of identity when dealing with government. The danger when there is an umbrella agency within government is that it is tempting for groups to come together with one voice and to coordinate their message. In the third sector and government, we should not lose the strong sense of integrity and identity that the various organizations can bring to the table, although it is more powerful, and thus tempting to agree to one message. A balance needs to be struck.

DEENA WHITE

That is an important question. In Quebec, social services are combined with health services in one ministry. The Ministry of Social Solidarity and Employment is the ministry of the poor. It deals with social assistance and employability development — a nice name for our version of workfare. There is a lot of significance in that. The secretariat is quite autonomous, although it is under that ministry. Under the new policy, it will likely be more autonomous. The new policy will be quite controversial because although it has an intersectoral view saying that all departments are going to go into their own partnerships with the third sector, this may also sectorize the community movement. Most groups in the community cannot see themselves as dealing with one ministry. They are much more holistic than that. Probably the most interesting and important thing is that the social economy is under the auspices of this ministry, it is funded by the Anti-Poverty Fund, and therefore it is created for the poor. The same can be said of the community action groups to a large extent in this vision. Therefore, while it is intersectoral and will bring in all ministries, it may have a tendency to create two classes of citizenship: those who can participate in society through the traditional labour market, accessing whatever public services remain and there are quite a few; and then the others who will participate in the social economy and will have access to services provided by community groups.

HAL GEREIN

In British Columbia, we are trying to achieve a relationship with the voluntary sector at the corporate level. This is not unlike the government relationship with the business sector. That relationship deals with the business sector at the corporate level including the regulatory interface — the relationship of how businesses are incorporated, shaped, taxed, and so on. It addresses how business relates to the full gamut of policies. The voluntary sector is seen as being a sector in its own right just as business is a sector in its own right. The ministry is charged with developing a relationship at that corporate level. We are interested in how organizations are constituted, how they report to their citizenry, what their requirements are to report back to government under the regulations, how the polices are working. There is an additional interest in the role of the sector in terms of community development, that is, their contribution to building healthy sustainable communities. This is not unlike the federal government in our view of the relationship to the sector.

LOUISE DELORME
Voluntary Sector Task Force
Privy Council Office

Too often we neglect what is happening in Quebec. There is a lot of innovation in Quebec, a lot of courage in how issues are approached there. We need more researchers to cover what is happening and then to integrate that research with what is being done in the rest of Canada. However, my question concerns the accreditation process under the project. How is this being handled? To what extent is there a contradiction between ensuring the autonomy of organizations and looking at their mandates and ensuring that there is a complementarity with government objectives if a group is to receive funding.

DEENA WHITE

The idea behind the accreditation process is to make departments responsible. One particular ministry or the Ministry of Social Solidarity and the Ministry of Health and Social Services, the two principle funders of the community groups, should not have to carry the whole load of funding. The hope is that by providing more core funding instead of project funding or funding specific services there would be some attenuation of this influence on the mandate of organizations funded. For example, they could not say to the groups that they can provide services but not advocacy. However, groups may share your concern and feel forced into the mould of a government department and how it defines its mandate. There are many groups who cannot define their mandate or activities within one or other sector of activity. Is an organization with its mandate labour force integration of persons with disabilities within Social Solidarity or Health and Social Services? Organizations will have difficulty defining their missions in accordance with the different departments (although the final policy allows for considerably more flexibility in this area).

BERNARD CHABOT
VOLNET Program
Industry Canada

Could you comment on the very different approach to voluntarism in Quebec? The current structure in Quebec gives the government influence over the organizations. On the other hand, the voluntary sector does not exist in Quebec, it is the community sector, instead. The new strategy is to work with service delivery. The effect of that strategy is to push away almost all the volunteers by pushing them into paid jobs.

DEENA WHITE

The community groups always have a position that is critical of what the government is doing. In fact the relationship is often called by different names, "contradictory participation," for example. "Cooperative conflict" is another. Under the system by which the workfare programs were run, welfare recipients were placed in community organizations. This tended to provide a lot of employees to these agencies, people who might otherwise have volunteered but now are paid. This is true. It is encouraged. It is part of the policy to create paid jobs. There is a tension between voluntarism and paid jobs. There is a political tension because many people feel that volunteers should be paid for their work, especially since the majority tend to be women. I do not have a comment about it other than to say that there is a tension there, but I do not see in Quebec the same concern to promote volunteerism as such. They talk about promoting participation but not about promoting volunteerism all that much. It is, however, the women's movement that is behind much of this sector in Quebec, and that may explain the scepticism about volunteering. It is more important that the unemployed have jobs with pay.

GUY FORTIN
Voluntary Sector Project Office
Treasury Board Secretariat

We have heard about the funding situation in Quebec. Would you comment on the funding issues in the other provinces? Is it a great concern within the sector?

HELEN HAYLES
Volunteer Centre of Winnipeg

I think sustainability is one of the most important issues facing the sector today. It is a concern, yes. Project funding has been nice, but it has left us without sustaining funding — the essential ingredient for continuing sector existence. This is the problem.

HAL GEREIN

I would echo that for British Columbia. It is a real problem. And as the government has tried to move to balanced or surplus budgets to deal with past spending, it reaches out and touches everybody. Particularly, it is felt within the community services sector where we feel we are getting more than the dollar for dollar invested. It is a tough issue, no doubt about it.

PANEL FOUR

MAKING THE RELATIONSHIP WORK: TWO CASE STUDIES

CASE ONE: FORGING A NEW MODEL FOR COLLABORATIVE GOVERNMENT-THIRD SECTOR ACTION: A STRATEGIC SOCIAL PLAN FOR NEWFOUNDLAND AND LABRADOR

PENELOPE ROWE
Executive Director
Community Services Council of Newfoundland and Labrador

It is quite fascinating for me that after all of these years of working on the Strategic Social Plan and in trying to encourage its development that this is the first time that I have actually been asked to make a formal presentation about it and it is the first time that Vivian Randell and I have tried to do a presentation together. She, of course, has the responsibility now for implementing the plan within the provincial government. I am going to talk about what predated the development of the Strategic Social Plan: how the concept was born within a community organization and how it led to the point in 1998 where the province released the Strategic Social Plan. Vivian will describe the plan itself. We will conclude by both offering some observations about where things stand currently and what some of the challenges and pitfalls and risks might be.

I represent a voluntary community-based organization that is a registered charity primarily focusing on social planning and social development. We have worked in a number of areas, including housing, child care, child abuse, and unemployment issues. At the point that our organization decided to try to encourage the provincial government to start concentrating on planning and its relationship with the voluntary sector, we were able to act with some credibility. When the Community Services Council was formed in 1975, one of its corporate objectives was to create a better relationship between governments and the voluntary sector. It was prescient of the group of citizens who formed the organization that they saw that as the primary motivation for our Social Planning Council. Not surprisingly then, the Strategic Social Plan in Newfoundland is not exclusively about a relationship with the voluntary sector but also about creating a framework for better development of social policy and better linking of social policy with economic policy. That was certainly a major part of the drive from the Community Services Council to initiating the Strategic Social Plan.

I will begin with the early stages of advocacy. The Community Services Council presents a brief on an annual basis to the Social Policy Committee of Cabinet. And in 1988, we decided that we had to encourage the government to take a more concrete, cohesive approach to social policy development and to its relationship with the voluntary sector and the organizations that the government funded. This idea was born, in part because we saw fragmented service delivery within the provincial government, a lack of relationship between departments and little interest in the delivery of social services except as last-resort programs. There was certainly a lack of understanding around the connections between economic development and social development. Instead, there existed a traditional mentality that the government had to get its fiscal house in order before concerning itself with social development and the work of the voluntary sector and priorities of the social departments. It was very much a residual, remedial approach, to social services and to social programming.

We initiated our advocacy by presenting a formal brief to the Social Policy Committee ministers. There was not much responsiveness to the notion of strategic social planning. The next year when my board asked me what we would present in our brief, I said that we would talk about strategic social planning and a framework for social policy development, but with a different tack. "Oh," they said. And then the following year when my board asked me again, I replied that we would continue talking about a strategic social plan. Along the way, Clyde Wells, who was a man of the traditional mindset that you should get the economic house in order and then think about social planning became the premier. As luck would have it, I was invited to speak at a Liberal policy convention where he was present. So I had him as captive audience for half an hour while I explained why the traditional thinking was wrong. We continued making our presentations to Cabinet and felt we were getting nowhere until one day in 1992, when I was leaving the premier's office on another matter he said, "By the way, the idea for a strategic social plan is going to be moved from the back burner to the front burner." A month later a commitment to develop the Strategic Social Plan was announced in the Throne Speech.

The premier had committed himself to the development of a strategic social plan. At this stage, the process became internal to government. The premier's first step was to establish a strategic planning group of deputy ministers. It was an exciting process because the group provided the opportunity for deputy ministers in any department with anything to do with social policy to come together and talk about issues of mutual concern. Although I was a rank outsider who was a very vocal community advocate, I was invited to join the group, which I suspect made some deputy ministers rather nervous. The other person who joined the group was the head of the Economic Recovery Commission, which was a government agency.

My challenge in the group then was multiple. First, I had to gain their trust. Second, I listened to them trying to work together, which was also a challenge because they did not have much of a relationship amongst themselves. Third, I had to convince them that there was a voluntary sector and that we had a significant role to play in the development of policy. So for two years, while the group worked, I continued to try to sell the concept of the voluntary sector. A fourth challenge presented itself in the preparation of a consultation document that was to go to the public. I was to write my section on the voluntary sector as if I were speaking from the perspective of government. That was a significant challenge because while I needed to be true to the sector; this was a government consultation paper. Another challenge was that I was the only person in the sector at the table and many of our discussions clearly were confidential. So there was some aggravation from other groups in the voluntary sector in the province about who I was and why I was at the table when they were not. Although they acknowledged that we had very firm relationships, they felt left out and wondered if they could trust me. This created some concern on my part.

Eventually the consultation paper was prepared for release, but by this time there was a transition to a new premier. He obviously wanted to review the paper before it was released to ensure that it suited his style. Fortunately for the process, he understood the concept of strategic social planning and had made a firm commitment in his election "red book" to developing a strategic social plan and engaging in public dialogue in advance of developing that plan. The premier then released the consultation paper and I was asked to chair the Social Policy Advisory Committee (SPAC) to convene public dialogue throughout the province. I explained to the premier that I wanted his authority to hold meetings with provincial civil servants in-camera so that they would feel free to express their views to our policy committee. It was my experience that many public servants knew what the problems were within government both in terms of fragmented service delivery and its relationship with the voluntary sector. It was clear to me that there were obviously different views at different levels within government, as well as between departments. The premier fortunately conceded to that request. Those in-camera discussions formed an important part of our process because throughout the public consultations we were able to balance the views we were hearing from the public, the voluntary sector, and people within government. It became clear that there was a high degree of consensus around what some of the critical issues were.

The SPAC committee had 14 members. It was a very strong community-based committee of nongovernmental people, mostly from the voluntary sector but also from health care and academe. Many of the people had been traditionally public advocates who were willing to tackle government. This spoke well to this process. A major challenge was getting this committee to work together effectively and to draw the committee into the vision about a new framework, to start moving beyond the traditional approach issues (whether it was issues of persons with disabilities or women's issues or issues for senior citizens), to the broader strategic framework. A further challenge in this process was that the consultation document was organized in a vertical manner and we wanted to move toward a structure that was more integrated and more horizontal.

The public dialogue process was very demanding. We met with stakeholders who represented each of the divisions as laid out in the consultation papers: social services, health, education, municipal affairs, the environment, women's issues, and housing, etc. Stakeholder meetings were by invitation and they allowed me to become well versed in what the issues were in health, in education, or in municipal affairs, and so on. But what began to happen as these groups came together and began to talk was the realization that they were all talking about very broad, similar themes. Very quickly cross-cutting themes began to emerge which were going to provide the basis for a strategic framework.

The framework consultations took place in 1996, which was one of the most difficult times in Newfoundland's history. The guts had gone out of the fishing industry because of the northern cod moratorium. Virtually every community we went into was in total and utter upheaval. People were losing their jobs, they had nowhere to turn, they were moving in busloads out of their communities. At 50 percent of the meetings, people were crying and were worried about what their future would hold. It was also tough on the people conducting the public consultation. I attended all the meetings. Other committee members were there on a volunteer basis and attended meetings as they could. Much of the productive work of the committee was, in fact, done in a car driving from meeting to meeting.

The consultation process was very successful because we used a wide array of consultation techniques. There was a great deal of scepticism and cynicism as we went around the province. People, hearing of the consultation would say, "Oh, one more of these road shows." People saw me as the "government's patsy" since I was chairing the process. The public was sceptical. It was important to build trust and to make people realize at the end of the day that what they were saying to us was going to be accepted and included in the documents that we prepared. Instead of going with the traditional consultation where we sat at a table and people came and presented briefs, we used every kind of public consultation process imaginable to build this trust. In most communities we brought people from all different sectors into a room and made them stay at a table while there was discussion. We also set up one-on-one discussions. If somebody had something they wanted to say privately, we would meet with them individually. We had our in-camera sessions with public servants. We had formal briefs for a number of volunteer organizations. In the end we had 1,500 representations that we had to give voice to.

The critical turning point came for the SPAC at the end of November, a Friday night. The committee had an important meeting to prepare for our first presentation to Cabinet on Monday morning. This was the most intensive two days. I sat with a group of people who were still thinking by sectors, by departments, and by issues that were important to each of us. Somehow the group had to get to the point where I was prepared to do an hour presentation to Cabinet. This was the turning point for our committee because it was the first time they would see me in action and know whether they could trust me in terms of what I would say to government. It turned out to be a successful meeting because we focused primarily on what we had heard from the public. It was a very distressing meeting because a lot of what we had heard was unpleasant. People, especially in rural communities, were really hurting. On the other hand, we were able to tell government that there were common themes and that the public was clearly willing to assume more responsibility, wanted more authority for local decision-making, and wanted to be more engaged in the policy process.

After the meeting with Cabinet on 1 December, the committee went back to the drawing board. How would we ever put this work together in a way that would represent the public, feel honest to the committee, and at the same time be something that the province could do. All these issues produced pressure because the government kept saying, "This has to be doable." Well, of course, it had to be doable. There was no point in preparing documents and recommendations that could not be handled.

One of the struggles was how to write a report that would meet these three imperatives. The report, in the end, produced a framework for social development. The committee decided to get rid of all the recommendations that were built around different sectors: social services, health, education. The primary recommendations in the document were around investing in people, building up community strengths and local assets, and integrating social and economic development. We also focused on the role of the voluntary sector and specific issues relating to children and youth.

The report was submitted to government in 1997. Shortly thereafter, it was jointly released by the premier and the committee. The premier said he would take it under advisement and two months later we learned that Cabinet had accepted the document "in principle." The report then disappeared into a big, dark hole and I went into withdrawal because I no longer had anything to do with what was going to come out at the other end.

This is where Vivian comes in. She was responsible for transforming the basic concept presented by SPAC to the Strategic Social Plan that government would ultimately release as its policy direction.

VIVIAN RANDELL
Assistant Secretary to Cabinet (Social Policy)

Once the Social Policy Advisory Committee (SPAC) had reported to government, a process was put in place to develop a policy instrument that would guide our social planning within the province. It is fair to say that the government's commitment at that time was still tenuous. There were significant concerns about how we were going to manage this process fiscally, and significant concerns about raised public expectations. So it was not at all certain that we were going to be able to produce a document that would not be treated as yet another government report and left on the shelf to gather dust.

In fact, we have succeeded in ways that perhaps none of us anticipated at the time, including a great deal of political commitment as well as commitment at the bureaucratic level. But this involvement had to be forged. One of the key factors in our ability to achieve a document of this nature certainly had to do with the fact that the future of the province was at stake. By 1996, we were very cognizant of the fact that our future was bleak and that if we did not find ways to pull together, as a province and as a people, we were going to have to surmount incredible obstacles and we were probably not going to succeed. Between 1992 and 1996 we lost around 12,400 full-time equivalent jobs. That was equal to 6.5 percent of our total employment and it was equal to the relative loss to Ontario of twice the size of its automobile industry and to British Columbia the loss of its entire forest industry. Our population declined between 1993 and 1998 by approximately 40,000 people. We dropped from a peak in 1993 of 586,000 to 540,000 in 1998. Media carried stories of every U-Haul truck in the entire province being rented. They were all on their way out of the province and crossing the gulf as families relocated. Communities were dying and we were aware of all the implications.

Here is a quick sense of some of the key highlights of the Strategic Social Plan once it was released in 1998 after a great deal of bureaucratic discussion and debate and much thoughtful consideration at the Cabinet level. One of the key communication challenges lay in convincing both the internal processes within government as well as the public that this was a long-term change strategy, that there were no immediate solutions and that we were concerned with reorganizing and engaging differently to address the issues facing the province. It was a commitment to integrating social and economic development and building on community and regional strengths. There was an impression among those of us within government following the SPAC report that we had to find ways to partner differently not only among ourselves but also with community and with the regional boards that were in place. The new emphasis had to be on population well-being with a focus on outcomes, and there were specific commitments to public accountability throughout the whole process.

The policy framework actually established visions, goals, and strategic directions that were intended to provide a backdrop for consensus-building throughout the province. Ministerial committees and deputy ministerial committees were established to guide the plan. Housing the administration of the plan within the Cabinet secretariat gave a clear signal that this process involved a corporate strategy that was to serve as a guide for all bureaucrats within government. We gave the responsibility to this central agency for ensuring that there was an integrated and coordinated approach taken through-out government.

Realizing the plan required certain policy shifts which we were committed to making, we knew it would be a challenge to build the culture with respect to those policy shifts. Even within our fiscal limitations we had to find ways to move from remedial crisis-driven approaches to more preventive and early in-tervention issues. For example, Newfoundland has one of the highest illiteracy rates in Canada. It was obvious to us that if we did not begin to address the issues of early childhood such as literacy, we were not going to succeed in the long term. There was a commitment to place-based development. This is the idea that communities must be looked at in the context of their viability and being able to access resources within a regional context. It also involved the question of how we were going to deal with the issues of social and economic infrastructure when we had so many small communities scattered throughout such a broad geographic range. There was a commitment to community capac-ity-building. We understood that this was partnering with the third sector in a very different fashion, that we had to recognize that healthy communities were the fundamental building blocks of economic development and if we did not have healthy communities (and certainly our communities were under incred-ible stresses), then we were not going to be able to attract economic develop-ment or industry in the future.

How have we strived to engage differently with the public and with the com-munity and what do we see as absolutely essential to the success of the plan? One of the initiatives in 1998 with the launch of the plan was the establishment of the Premier's Council on Social Development. Twenty people with diverse backgrounds from various sectors across the province were appointed to the council. The purpose of the council was to engage with government directly on the issues of policy development. It would be consulted on a regular basis and was intended to provide another lens through which government could examine the particular issues that it was addressing.

The council has been meeting since 1998, and it has been a struggle. The members have made it clear that they do not want to be used as window dress-ing, that they want a real and legitimate role in public policy. We have worked very carefully to build a strong relationship with deputy ministers in all de-partments and to help them understand the role of the council. It is clear that deputy ministers are accountable for bringing issues, especially major policy issues, to the table early in the game so that the council can influence the decision-making process and have an impact on the development of particular policies.

Demonstration project funding was established. It was intended to allow for some early success, but also to signal our recognition that we had to show community groups and the public our commitment to this new direction in social policy. In the first year we invested approximately $1.2 million in demonstration project funding. It was not always believed to be the best approach, but it was agreed that it was the first time that community agencies had been able to compete for a significant amount of government funding. The funding was tied to some of the things we were trying to achieve within the plan.

One of the key things that we have accomplished is that we have moved the plan from the drawing board and have made an effort to initiate a different kind of partnership in the community and regions. In many parts of the country it is an accepted practice to have regional boards delivering major public services. Newfoundland has a range of 44 boards throughout the province to deliver health institutions, public health, and community services, education including postsecondary; and there is a group involved in regional economic development. What is different is that we have brought these boards to a common table, with a surprising amount of success and commitment. They represent the local leadership. They have, within their bailiwicks, a substantial amount of government resources. Over half of the provincial government budget is at the regional board level. And finally, we realized that when we talk about coordinating social and economic development within government, we require a similar way to talk about those issues at the regional level. The various groups have come together and have begun exploring, implementing, and planning from a common approach.

Although there were many issues related to the different geographical boundaries of the various boards, we have succeeded now in creating six regions in the province. Some boards are participating in more than one region, but doing it willingly and they now meet regularly. Two regions are up and running and a third has started in Labrador. The other three are ready to look at the implementation of the Strategic Social Plan in their regions. The challenges facing these regional steering committees involve two key questions: How do we cooperate around common issues? What flexibility have we got to be able to address these issues?

One of the things that is of significant interest when we talk about the Strategic Social Plan is that we have established an accountability structure and a management information tool that we think is going to be extremely helpful in the process. Our Newfoundland Statistics Agency, with a lot of cooperation from Statistics Canada, developed a Web-site-based community information system. We now have information on 400 of our 700 communities in the province. We have subregional information that is available at the click of a computer mouse. The information system allows us to obtain specific community data, regional data, and provincially-based data on a range of indicators. Right now we have over 40,000 tables on the site. It is being used both as a planning tool and to support a social audit. The social audit involves a commitment to a public document that will provide information on the social landscape drawn from that Web site, evaluate a number of programs within government in terms of their actual outcomes, and offer valuable insight on whether we have successfully changed the way in which we do business. The first report is due in 2003 and the Premier's Council has played an active role in developing the framework for that particular document.

PENELOPE ROWE

One of the points of interest is how closely the Strategic Social Plan, ultimately released by the government, mirrors the framework put forward by the Social Policy Advisory Committee. Of course, there are some variations but the committee report was just a framework written in a tight, clean, short manner. As a result, the government had to put flesh around the framework and created a much stronger relationship between the people who designed the idea, the public and the voluntary sector, and the final product.

PENELOPE ROWE AND VIVIAN RANDELL

The continuing challenges involve:

- building trust and managing tensions;
- clarifying roles and responsibilities;
- balancing accountability and flexibility;
- finding ways to move forward together since substantive issues may defy resolution;
- financial limitations;
- adjusting to the impacts of the process and implementation of the Strategic Social Plan; and,
- responding to public concerns.

We are working together to meet these challenges.

CASE TWO: BUILDING CURA FROM THREE PERSPECTIVES

PETER LEVESQUE
Programme Officer
Social Sciences and Humanities Research Council

How did the Community-University Research Alliance, known as CURA, come about? What have been the results to date? And how has this program changed the thinking at the Social Science and Humanities Research Council (SSHRC), which is an arm's length agency of Industry Canada.

CURA is an example of social entrepreneurship. What do I mean by that? I mean that CURA exists because of people like Penny Rowe or Tim Brodhead of the McConnell Foundation who both serve on the SSHRC Council telling us what they mean, what they want, what their ideas are, and how they can be implemented. The program that preceded CURA was CRIC (Community Research and Information Crossroads). CRIC has supported hundreds of people who are engaged in many different types of research. Canadians, however, did not invent this. CURA has its lineage in science shops in Europe, starting as a student movement in the 1970s and continuing today. In fact, the European Union through the quotas program funds something called Improving Human Potential and they are looking at the science shops as a model to transfer to other European countries. CURA also has its roots in the idea that research funded by a democratic society should be democratic and should respond to the needs of its population. Interesting idea. So CURA is a program that was born out of this social entrepreneurship.

When I was asked to take on CURA as a program officer, I had 152 questions. I took it apart, some of it made sense and some not, and there are still improvements coming. But two cautionary principles were introduced. One was from Francis Fukyama's book entitled *Trust*.[1] He says that governments

---

[1] Francis Fukuyama, *Trust: The Social Virtues and the Creation of Prosperity* (New York: Free Press, 1995).

are really good at creating programs that use up social capital, but they are not very good at creating programs that help build up social capital. I wanted to make sure that this program was not one of those. The other one was from a senior public servant who said, "governments are bad partners. Priorities change, people change and so if you are going to be involved in this process, how do you be a good partner?" These were the two precautionary principles.

The CURA program does something quite simple. It has a broad mandate that says, "Help organizations within communities and university institutions combine forces and tackle issues that you have identified as being a common priority concern." It currently provides up to $600,000 a year for funding in three areas of activity: research, education and training, and dissemination. The support structures were built around those three areas. CURA is different from any other program we fund because payments are made in the first competition not only to universities but also to organizations like the McCord Museum, the Thames Valley Children's Centre, or the Youth Services Bureau of Ottawa Carleton. They are the lead investigators and they have university partners, and that surprised university research offices. In the first round, we expected 60 to 70 applications. We received 178 letters of intent. David Armour, president of the United Way, said, "If we thought you were serious, you would have gotten ten times the applications." Two-thousand applications would cause our entire system to crash but it woke us up to the realization of how important this process is. We were struck by the volume of research in the community, the quality of ideas, and most importantly, how drastic the need is for research that relates to what is being done within the communities daily.

The 178 applications were adjudicated by an impressive committee that included members of the Order of Canada, university researchers, community-based agencies representatives, foundation representatives, business representatives — a broad sector. Seventy-five applications were invited back, 72 were submitted as full applications and 22 were funded. They ranged from proposals for creating a centre for alternative dispute resolution at the University of British Columbia Law School to proposals intended to develop sustainable fisheries management on the east coast between native and non-native fishers. The same thing happened when we created a sister program called "CAHR," Canadian Alliances for Health Research. That program received 180 applications. In the 2000 CURA competition, we received 120 applications and invited back 34, with funding for up to 15. When we started this program we were going to fund eight in each year and council members protested that "This is ridiculous. We have to fund more." So the budget was tripled in the first year, doubled it in the second and there is an agreement to extend the pilot program beyond the first two years. To give you an appreciation of the scope of information processed in CURA, I read through 8,000 pages of supporting documents and received 27,400 emails, phone messages and letters over two years!

How is it affecting the thinking of SSHRC? Well, the fact that this program exists at all is a huge indication that the thinking is changing: writing a cheque to a community-based organization with research as part of its mandate is a huge change. This says that SSHRC funds research, not necessarily researchers. The difference is subtle but important. Research happens all over the place: within community-based organizations, both because of need but also because it enables them to perform their functions better. Research develops capacity. The new program launched in the nonprofit sector in Canada is the same thing. Any proposal can be submitted. It must be good research, but there is also the recognition that good research happens in places other than universities.

What else is happening? We are soliciting input. This is very different. We are trying to close the loop on research. Before, proposals would be submitted and adjudicated, cheques were sent out, the final productivity report came in, and we launched a new program, etc. CURA is trying to close the loop so that research that is being funded is not only useable and *is* being used by the communities and universities, but that feedback is provided to SSHRC in order to guide improvements to existing programs as well as the creation of new ones. This will ensure that we are continually more responsive. Another indication of how thinking has changed is that in the federal government mini-budget, SSHRC got another $100 million over the next five years. That is a huge amount of money!

KATHERINE GRAHAM
Associate Dean
Faculty of Public Affairs and Management
Carleton University

It is a pleasure to discuss my involvement with CURA. My place in all of this is, in a sense, in the middle. If cheques were sent to individuals, SSHRC would have sent me a cheque since my name is on the CURA application for the voluntary sector evaluation research project as the lead person from Carleton

University. Having said that, I do not really have a "hands-on" role in the research itself. The research is a collaboration between Carleton and our principal researcher Susan Phillips, with the Canadian Centre for Philanthropy and Michael Hall as the other co-principal investigator along with a number of national voluntary organizations and community-based networks. This is really what is interesting and potentially significant about CURA.

Our project is titled the Voluntary Sector Evaluation Research Project or VSERP, which some think is a slick new sports drink. The idea is to try to build the capacity of the sector by looking at the evaluation processes that it currently undertakes at the community, intermediate, and national levels, identifying gaps, and developing and testing new approaches that will help augment the capacity of the sector to undertake evaluation. Involved in VSERP as committed partners are not only national organizations representing the sector such as Volunteer Canada, United Way of Canada/Centraide Canada, YMCA Canada, and of course, the Canadian Centre for Philanthropy, but we also have a couple of funders or organizations that are interested in the funding end of things, notably the Max Bell Foundation and the Canadian Comprehensive Auditing Foundation now known as CCAF. We are an eclectic group, which leads to an interesting life together.

The process of putting VSERP together was very challenging in the sense that it involved a coming together of the national partners. Michael Hall started to talk to Susan Phillips who talked to Sol Kasimir of YMCA Canada, who talked to Dave Armour of the United Way/Centraide Canada, and on it went. It very quickly became evident that if we were to do something practical we had to think not only in terms of national, but also at the grassroots level.

I want to talk about the lessons learned from my perspective as the associate dean at Carleton responsible for managing the CURA from the university's perspective. My observations fit within three domains. First are the lessons learned from engaging at the local level and Tim Simboli will continue with this. Second, lessons learned from engaging with diverse national organizations and I have alluded to this as part of the foundation of the CURA. Third, lessons learned inside the university. I will discuss the first two briefly and will go into the lessons learned inside the university in more depth.

First, lessons from engaging at the local level. The most striking thing for me is the two vocabulary problem. The fact is, as you talk with community-based voluntary organizations, you must immediately take a leap of faith and establish a platform of trust. I recall vividly a meeting attended by a number of local voluntary organizations as we were putting together the proposal. The meeting was designed not only to brief them on what we were trying to do but to also get their support. I made a presentation and it was clear that what I was talking about was maybe resonating to some degree with what people's needs and interests were, but the language I was using was not right. I was speaking the language of SSHRC and these people were using the language of working on the street. At the conclusion of the meeting, I asked whether, in the course of the discussions, they had developed enough trust in me to feel that I would represent their issues through the proposal process. I hoped that I had heard what people were saying but that it was important to use language familiar to SSHRC in the proposal. We did get the letters of support and we were successful.

The second lesson came from engaging diverse national organizations. One of the things from the standpoint of any university that wants to engage with the voluntary sector at the national level and is that we cannot play favourites. It is very important for universities not to think that there is a perfect partner out there to go to first and then to sit back and see how the politics plays out. Having said that, I think it is modestly possible for universities to play a convening role with national organizations in the sector and to bring them together.

And third, lessons are learned inside the university. There really is a need to consciously manage community-based research with the sector within the university. It is not just a research role. There is a management role involved and the reason why it exists is because of the almost infinite demands on the sector, particularly at the community level. For example, the good news is that we were successful and received CURA funding. What are we going to use this money for? Well the sector, at the local level particularly, is so starved for resources that it would be easy to say, "Well we are going to use the CURA money for this need or for that because there is a need." There must be a managed way within the university of stepping back and saying, "Okay. What activities are really consistent with the research design here? This research project is about community capacity-building, but it is not about doing everything for the community."

The second thing, and this is somewhat related, is that there are the challenges of making different appetites for research and research agendas work collaboratively within the university. We have colleagues within Carleton who are engaged with our project and who are interested in policy and are potentially or already making great contributions to policy thinking about the sector. We also have people who are rooted in the community, with different goals for research. The challenge is to bring them together and to have them work constructively so that we do the most with our engagement with the sector. This is not easy.

The third thing that we need to think about in the university is that we should learn from our experience through CURA. At Carleton we are learning. Our experience with CURA has given us valuable lessons in order to apply for other SSHRC-based grants with a community focus.

TIMOTHY SIMBOLI
Executive Director
Ottawa-Carleton Family Service Centre

The Family Service Centre is an average size community-based agency. That means we have about 50 professional staff and an annual budget of $2.2 million. We are certainly not a large, well-known organization. We have never been rich. We are not very well publicized. We have been cutting corners throughout the 1990s and right now we are rather like a yellow packaged, no frills operation. On the other hand, we are dedicated. Nobody in their right mind would work in our organization for the wages we pay. And we are effective. Our client ratings, which we do on a regular basis, are embarrassingly high. And we are fairly typical in that we are not terribly typical of anybody else in the sector.

There is so much uniqueness among organizations that I have often struggled to find out what we mean by the third sector, who does it include, who doesn't it include? And once you draw parameters around that, what do we actually share? I say that as a caveat to my remarks. We need to understand those cultural differences at the fundamental level of organizational philosophy. It is truly well beyond the issues of community-university research, but I think that it is instructive here. So I will present a fairly subjective observation of the work in Ottawa.

First, let me explain what we are trying to do in Ottawa. We call ourselves the Community-Based Research Network of Ottawa. Our group does not see ourselves as conducting research per se but rather enabling it to happen and promoting its use and values. We are concerned with research in its broadest sense, outcome evaluation, best practices, cost-benefit analysis, etc. We endorse that broad definition of research that we heard at the beginning of this case study. Simply put, we hope to assist community-based agencies in finding answers to their questions. The work on university-community collaboration in Ottawa has been going on for some time. We are fortunate enough to have two universities and two colleges in the area that connect themselves with the community in a number of ways. There have been many staff crossovers into the community and back into academia. There are student placements in many organizations. There is mutual involvement in social and other issues. This activity provided the background for our discussions and over the last few years, a group of university and community personnel got together and started to talk about this. There is a real value in putting a group of people in a room, not giving them an agenda and then seeing what emerges.

Our discussions started informally and then became more organized in the mid- to late nineties. A few of us from the community agencies were actually university-trained researchers who had a parallel occupation in the community so we had some crossover ideas. We felt that there was a lot being done in the research field but that much of it was missing the mark. It really was not the kind of research studies that we could take off the shelf and give to our staff and have them use.

Also involved in these discussions were people from the university and they were interested in seeing their students become more connected, able to make better contributions when they came out of school. The staff and the leadership of the School of Social Work in Carleton University deserves a lot of credit for engaging and committing to the research placements. Now that is not unique within that particular school, but it certainly was that strong commitment carried on over time that was really important. I also think that the emphasis on context and power analysis and communication that is found in a social work discipline has provided some of the background that has made these discussions worthwhile.

In this form, for this particular initiative, the discussions really began in 1998 in earnest in a more formal way. There have been 15 to 20 regular participants from the community and the university. We spent a lot of time sorting out and articulating our feelings and our thoughts, what we were going to do, identifying what was missing and expanding on those, arguing over what should be done, and what could be done. At that point, as would be expected, everybody did what they normally do. The academics went off and did a literature search, and the community people went looking for money. Have you been looking for money? It sounds funny because there was a caricature of the way we perceive ourselves but what worked and drew us together was seeing the wisdom of each other's actions. It really was combining the strengths and finding that complementarity. We had a notion that we would be a clearinghouse or a roundtable for community-based research. We would enable field research by helping put together interesting people with research questions from their field with people interested in research and maybe connecting them with some suitable resources. Broader than that, we would provide a forum for promoting first the value of research knowledge within the third sector at the grassroots level, and second, the importance of conducting research that answers meaningful questions among the academics. We faced a number of hurdles.

Well-meaning people who are extremely busy sometimes have a great deal of trouble maintaining momentum. Finding the resources to conduct some of the labour has been a very thorny issue. We had struggled in bootstrapping this project when we bumped into the SSHRC initiative and it really was a very serendipitous event. We discovered that we had a really strong thread that wove very nicely into what was going on at CURA. We insinuated ourselves into the national project and that is exactly how it worked.

Let me just go off on a bit of a tangent here. The funding that has come through is project funding obviously and there was a comment earlier about the critical nature of project funding. I just wanted to say that I find project funding to be a little like pushing drugs. The agencies become addicted to it. We expand our programs, we employ new staff and then the program ends, the project is over. It is great for us in that we use it for research and development but when it ends we have labour problems and we have financial problems. It should be remembered that the third sector, the community agencies, are, I was going to say impoverished, but it is probably more that we are malnourished. Research is seen as a luxury. It is not something that we can do and do easily. All our resources go into the mandate and the mission for the agencies. Oftentimes research in organizations equates to outcome evaluation, that sort of necessary but very evil part of funding. Helping research happen includes providing the means to do research, obviously. So being inventive and creative and finding resources is something that organizations can bring to the table.

I mentioned earlier that finding time and maintaining energy was problematic, particularly for the community-based individuals since many were already stretched to incredible limits. They found it hard to make meetings consistently. We assigned tasks already and shared the workload. We had trouble making sure that we were producing the kind of work that was needed or the quality that we needed. We ended up becoming very tolerant of each other and our abilities to try and blend our schedules and not always meeting the deadlines. It makes management of the project an absolute nightmare and that became Katherine Graham's problem. She mentioned working in the common language and in Ottawa that usually means you have to work in both English and French, but it was a really professional language that needed to be sorted out. We had lengthy discussions around acronyms. It was unbelievable. But below the language we needed to understand the relationships among the players in our sectors. We needed to educate each other. And there were the dynamics and priorities of our work, and below that the values and philosophical underpinnings of our sectors and our professions. This took time but it was very necessary.

The complication is that as you build synergy you run the risk of developing "group-think" and so we often played devil's advocate or had a team "B" approach. If we had an idea, someone would go away and write a critique. The power balance has been mentioned as being crucial and I think this is very important. Community agencies, by and large, are entering the area of research feeling woefully inadequate on many, many levels. That is why research often does not happen in community-based agencies. We have trouble doing it. It is easy and very detrimental to the process that in that kind of an environment the community-based agencies take a one-down position almost from the beginning and it means that you have to put your thumb on the scale to bring that back up. The issuing of cheques to community agencies is a good idea.

So let me come up with a couple of conclusions here. I see some parallels all the way up the line to the national level. Beyond this there are some really compelling reasons to do research. We need information. There is no point making any of the philosophical or theoretical or strategic decisions unless we have really good, sound information to base them on. Research provides some of that. It can come from other places as well. I draw the analogy that Ottawa is a hotbed of high-tech firms right now and a measure of their strength is the amount of money that they put into their research and development. If it is a strong commitment, 10 to 15 percent, that seems a strong company with a strong future and right now we do not spend very much doing research and development in our sector at all.

I work with kids and there is some really informative literature out there on the resilient child. What makes kids survive really awful situations? Take children in disasters, give them an opportunity to participate, have them believe that somebody else cares about them and give them a sense of well-being that comes from a sense of competence. And if you do that, kids will thrive. We can learn from this.

SELECTED COMMENTS FROM THE DISCUSSION

JOHN O'LEARY
President
Frontier College

A number of speakers alluded to dialogue or consultation fatigue. I wonder if people might want to comment about research fatigue. I do not mean to be glib since people have also said how important research is. Frontier College, a literacy organization, was founded in 1899 and at that time the teachers taught loggers and miners. Today we work in inner city communities.

I was recently at a meeting with a university, a foundation, and a school board and they wanted to do research about possible links between poverty and school failure. So they are doing this important research. Are there any comments on how to deal with this type of situation?

KATHERINE GRAHAM

From my perspective as part of a community organization engaged in research and with a long relationship with university researchers, I have not ascertained that there is research fatigue. I would suggest that perhaps we are not very good at using what we find in our research in a way that people can understand and use and see that it is going somewhere. Sometimes research is done for the sake of doing research, but even so there are often many issues that are important. We do not put enough time into any of our daily lives for public discourse and dissemination of the research information. I think we do our work and then move on to something else. This is due in part to project funding and partly to the way in which most of us operate.

One of the things that I have observed in various discussions with community-based organizations is not so much research fatigue but lack of recognition of the fact that there is a huge activity of research in the sector at the local level. So we label something research with a capital R and it is something that has to result in an article in a refereed journal. In fact, there is a huge amount of research that takes place in many community-based organizations. There may or may not be merit in looking at the link between poverty and school outcomes. But my view is that there is a huge amount of merit in trying to mine the research that is already there. It may be something by another name, but we need to look at what we have because we do not really know what we do have.

PETER LEVESQUE

When we talk in terms of closing the loop, we are simply trying to make sure that the information produced from projects we fund is disseminated and transferred to as many places as possible. A successful CURA application involves at least 100 person-days of work to bring it forward. This is unacceptable. Therefore, we are examining mechanisms to fund more proposals and make sure that it is good research, good teaching, and good dissemination, and to improve the process for getting the money. The application fatigue is reduced and researchers can actually do their work.

DIANNE BASCOMBE
Executive Director
Ottawa-Carleton Centre for Voluntary Sector Research and Development

Just for purposes of learning, I think it would be useful if the panelists might reflect on aspects of the collaboration that have failed because every collaboration has unfulfilled promises and I think that is an important part of what case studies can teach us.

PENELOPE ROWE

At this stage in our process in Newfoundland, whether it was the process that I was engaged in, or where the provincial government and its partnerships are at the moment, our primary weakness is that there are a number of groups who are not engaged. We still have to involve more organizations in the process. That is part of what is in the works but it is going to take a long time to get there. With reference to the ultimate impact of the Strategic Social Plan on the voluntary sector, it is not going to address some of the key issues that we know were of concern to the sector such as the lack of stability, and some insecurity. The other piece from my point of view is the misunderstanding about what we mean when we talk about the voluntary sector, particularly from the perspective of the labour movement and their concern that this is all about just another way of downloading. We need to find the time to dispel that idea when it should be dispelled or to deal with it when it should be dealt with. And certainly at a local community level one of the issues will continue to be the people moving in and out of being volunteers to being paid employees. This is not all captured in our plan even though we are kind of nibbling at some of these things.

My main point is really about the fragility of the process and how dependent any process like this is on key individuals. If those individuals move on, I think there are always serious risks of processes falling apart, getting this process through has been very dependent on having the right people in the right places. Our challenge now so that we do not fail is making sure that the buy-in gets beyond a few of those key people whom we have acknowledged we need as champions. If it is going to really be internalized and be part of the way in which we all change the way we do business, I think it is going to have to be understood by a much broader group of people.

KATHERINE GRAHAM

I think it is too early to talk about absolute failure yet, which is the optimist in me. But I will say that there is at least one major snake in the weeds and that is that the demand for research on issues that affect the sector is so great and we have a very focused agenda — in itself it is broad. We are trying to develop evaluation resources and capacity for the sector, but it is not the big picture and so the challenge for us will be to keep expectations proportionate to what we can do and hope that we are successful in doing that because otherwise the danger is that there is an even greater credibility gap than already exists between the academy and community-based organizations in the sector.

VIVIAN RANDELL

In terms of the process that we are engaged in and embarked on, failure really looms large all the time. One thing that I have found very heartening about the process is the degree to which people have come together and said, "We have tried to be very honest in the relationship in the sense of saying to people at a community level, We cannot promise that all of the decisions of government will meet with the kinds of principles that we are articulating here. We cannot control all the factors that impact upon the kinds of issues that we are dealing with. But essentially, we feel that there is a benefit to beginning the conversation and seeing where it takes us." I also have to say I have no idea where this is taking us. I have always had an affinity for that kind of description of organizing which essentially says, "We may not know where we are going until we get there." The process is messy and so do not panic in the face of disorder and understand that sometimes we have to engage in the impossible in order to figure out what is possible. I think that is essentially the kind of process that we are involved in right now. And in some respects what is interesting is that I am not sure now that even if government wanted to dissociate itself from the process that we can stop what we have started. A discussion has begun and it will have ramifications.

TIMOTHY SIMBOLI

We have covered a lot of the difficulties that we are facing and I think overarching all these are problems of patience, having too much and having too little.

PETER LEVESQUE

Sometimes a failure is strictly one of communication. Take the difference between proposals from the medical community and the natural sciences and engineering and the social sciences and humanities. When you ask the voting public, "Do you want a new medication, a new bridge, or a postmodern explanation of why hospital lines are too long?" What do you think they will take? Part of the challenge, and it is an opportunity, is to explain why you need information that discusses why hospital lines are too long and what some of the potential solutions are. A lot of people are listening right now. There is clear recognition that practical social sciences and humanities research is a priority. Some failures are strictly a matter of communication. You just need to find better ways of communicating and continuing to communicate. What will we talk about this year? This year, same thing. Next year, same thing. Eventually people begin to hear the message.

PANEL FIVE

ENGAGING IN THE POLICY PROCESS: CHALLENGES FOR THE THIRD SECTOR

MICHAEL HALL
Vice President Research
Canadian Centre for Philanthropy

Opportunities and Challenges of the Third Sector

With recent government interest in the voluntary sector, we have the opportunity to help increase the social and economic contributions that voluntary organizations can make to the lives of Canadians. I would like to present the findings of recent research that show that public opinion about voluntary organizations is favourable. I will argue that this favourable public opinion, coupled with new government interest in the voluntary sector, provides a positive environment for initiatives to improve the capacity of voluntary organizations to provide benefits to Canadians. There are, however, a number of challenges that we will need to overcome in order to develop policy that will help to improve voluntary sector capacity.

One challenge is the lack of knowledge we have about voluntary organizations. We know surprisingly little because there has been limited research on this important set of institutions. This lack of knowledge limits our ability to develop sound policy. At present, voluntary sector policy initiatives can only be based on anecdotes and stereotypes. We need to move beyond developing policy based on our own particular beliefs and experiences toward developing policy that is based on a solid understanding of the voluntary sector. Also, there is a lack of conceptual frameworks to guide thinking about the role that voluntary organizations play in modern society.

Another challenge arises from the lack of clearly specified targets for the current policy initiatives associated with the Voluntary Sector Initiative (VSI). This may be appropriate given our current lack of knowledge; but, as we start to move forward, we will need more precision to ensure that we do not miss an opportunity to improve the contributions that these organizations are making.

Let me start by discussing some of the latest public opinion research regarding the voluntary sector. This research comes from a study that the Canadian Centre for Philanthropy conducted for the Muttart Foundation in the summer of 2000.[1] We tried to get a sense of what people think about charities, a subset of voluntary organizations registered with the Canada Customs and Revenue Agency. These findings provide a fairly good picture of what public opinion about voluntary organizations, in general, is likely to be. The study explored what people think about charities and the roles they play, as well as the trust people have in these organizations.

We posed a few key questions. First, we asked people the extent to which they agreed or disagreed that charitable organizations are becoming increasingly important to many Canadians. Almost 90 percent agreed that charitable organizations are becoming increasingly important. We also asked this question in the negative to ensure that we had a robust sense of the perceived importance of charities. Only about 30 percent indicated that charitable organizations do *not* do much to improve the quality of life for Canadians.

We examined how charities are viewed vis-à-vis government. Almost 80 percent of Canadians indicated that charitable organizations understand the needs of the average Canadian better than government does. Based on these results, I would suggest that there is likely to be public support to current initiatives that are bringing voluntary organizations into the policy process.

Close to 70 percent of those surveyed believe that charities do a better job than government in meeting the needs of Canadians. These data suggest that there may be a willingness among Canadians to entertain a greater role for charities in that aspect of their work. On a cautionary note, 74 percent of Canadians do not want charities to be a substitute for government services.

---

[1] M.H. Hall, L. Greenberg and L. McKeown, *Talking about Charities: Canadians' Opinions on Charities and Issues Affecting Charities* (Edmonton: The Muttart Foundation, 2000) (available at >www.nonprofitscan.org>).

Our study also explored the perceptions of the role that charities have in advocating for specific policies. Eighty-eight percent of those surveyed agreed that charities should speak out on issues like the environment, poverty or health care. In addition, almost 50 percent indicated that there should not be any limits placed on the advocacy functions of charities. It should be noted that charities are limited to devoting 10 percent of their resources to advocacy. Of those who think there should be limits, very few believe it should be less than 10 percent. These results indicate that there would be support among many Canadians for an increased advocacy role for charities.

Canadians appear to have a high level of trust in charities. When we asked about the general level of trust in charitable organizations, 77 percent of Canadians said they trusted them "some" or "a lot." We tried to get a sense of the relative level of trust in charities by probing which professions are trusted most. Only doctors and nurses are trusted more than people working in charities.

One of the issues that is being addressed by the Voluntary Sector Initiative is the capacity of voluntary organizations to undertake their work. Our study indicates that Canadians believe that charities do not have enough funding to do the work they do. Almost 60 percent indicate that charities have too little money to do their work, suggesting that there is likely to be public support for initiatives to improve the financial resources of voluntary organizations.

All in all, I think it is fair to say that we have a very favourable policy environment for the voluntary sector. There is government interest and initiatives at both the federal and provincial levels. The public recognizes the value of these organizations. They have a high level of trust in what charities are doing and they recognize that these organizations need resources. But, as I have indicated, there are challenges. We may miss the mark in what may be a "once in a lifetime opportunity" to develop policies that can help to increase the contributions that voluntary organizations make to Canadian society.

There are a number of reasons that current policy initiatives may be suboptimal. One reason is that the policy objectives that are being established lack precision. For example, the VSI is intended "to increase the capacity of the voluntary sector to meet the demands Canadian society places on it" and "to improve the government's policies, programs and services to Canadians." The Ontario government's initiative of a few years ago was intended "to strengthen volunteerism and improve the quality of life of Ontarians." These are very broad policy statements and people are discovering that virtually anything can take place under them.

Deena White's presentation about initiatives underway in Quebec provides a good example of more specified policy objectives that are targeting nonprofits with a social mission anchored in the community. This is a preferable approach in that it is beginning to narrow the scope of initiatives and to make sure it is targeted in a particular area. Hopefully, there will be more specificity as the recommendations begin to be developed at the various joint tables that are working within the VSI.

At present, however, we are working without clear definitions of what the target of all of this policy work is. I am troubled by the lack of a conceptual framework for this sector, by the lack of clear, common definitions, and by the somewhat murky terminology. Now some may say that the voluntary sector is messy and we should be comfortable with it like that. The sector may indeed be messy, but our thinking about it needs to be more systematic.

For example, few of the presentations have defined their subject. We have heard about the third sector, about nonprofits, and about voluntary organizations. We have heard about the civil society sector, community-based organizations, and so on. Is the civil society sector the same as the voluntary sector, or the same as the nonprofit sector? I would argue that they are not the same. They are different things in many respects. Each one of these terms comes from a different discipline. Each has a slightly different nuance and yet we seem to be using these terms interchangeably. When we talk, each one of us is talking about something else, but we do not know precisely what that something else is. Until we start to adopt some common definitions, we are going to have difficulty developing good policy. To a social scientist, this conceptual confusion is an indication of an early stage of inquiry. Until we start to develop some common language we are not going to be able to move the policy process along.

We can view the voluntary sector as a pyramid. At the base are the approximately 870,000 grassroots organizations (this is a rough estimate based on David Horton Smith's estimation of the density of associational life in the United States as being 30 per 1,000 people). At the next level are 100,000 nonprofits (as estimated by Jack Quarter at OISE). At the top of the pyramid are the 78,000 charities that are registered with the Canada Customs and Revenue Agency. What comprises the base of this pyramid? These are the grassroots associations, self-help organizations, ratepayers' associations, protest groups, parks associations, and sports and hobby clubs. All of these are formalized in that they meet, they may have a constitution, and they may have meetings, but they cannot own anything because they are not incorporated. They engage in a variety of activities, often at the local level and they may be relatively impermanent. This grassroots base is likely to be the incubator for the incorporated organizations. As groups gain some permanence, they may decide that they should rent an office or employ staff. This will usually lead them to incorporate so that the person who takes out the lease or hires an employee is not personally liable for the activities of the group. The organization may then become a nonprofit, incorporated organization, one of the 100,000 or so organizations toward the peak of the pyramid. Finally, if they are working in one of the five areas of activity that qualifies them for registered charity status in the eyes of the Canada Customs and Revenue Agency (religion, education, health, relief of poverty or other areas of benefit to the public), then they will be able to issue tax receipts for donations and they will move up to the top of the pyramid, joining the other 78,000 charities.

When we talk about the voluntary sector in our policy debates, are we referring to all of these organizations? From a public policy perspective, there may be interest in the base of the pyramid because these organizations are likely to be engaged in a lot of advocacy work and the provision of some community services. They are also the incubator for the more formal, incorporated organizations. However, if government interest in the voluntary sector lies with assisting organizations that can provide services on behalf of government then the policy focus will be toward the peak of the pyramid among those organizations that are incorporated. It is, perhaps, no coincidence that current public policy privileges charities (those at the peak) because these organizations work in areas in which governments have historically also had an interest — health, education, and social welfare.

When we use the term "nonprofit organization" in discourse, we are excluding the 870,000 grassroots or unincorporated organizations because nonprofits are typically defined as having a non-distribution constraint and they are incorporated. However, the nonprofit category includes a variety of organizations such as trade associations, NAV Canada (which was created by government to run our airports), professional associations, as well as organizations like the Vancouver Immigrant Women's Society.

From a policy perspective, how does one deal with the diversity of organizations that co-exist within the boundaries connoted by the term nonprofit organizations? Should all of these organizations be treated the same? Are we interested in them equally? Perhaps not. A distinction is often made between mutual benefit and public benefit organizations. Many nonprofit organizations have been created to serve the benefit of their members (e.g., social clubs, trade associations). However, many mutual benefit organizations also provide public benefits. For example, the Canadian Nurse's Association and the

Canadian Medical Association are mutual benefit organizations which also make broader societal contributions.

The term "civil society" denotes a much broader set of organizations. For-profit entities may be included in civil society if they are working toward pro-social ends. In addition, some of these work in partnership with voluntary organizations to provide social benefits.

Each of these terms — voluntary organization, nonprofit organization or civil society — implies a different set of boundaries and a different set of organizations. For the development of policy it is important, however, to have a clear sense about where policy initiatives are being targeted. If the policy concerns advocacy, then the entire pyramid is a legitimate target. If the interest is citizen engagement, efforts should be targeted at the grassroots that form the base of the pyramid. If the interest is service delivery then nonprofits or, perhaps, charities should be targeted.

There is tremendous diversity within each of these three types of organizations that also needs to be recognized, particularly if the policy initiatives being developed are intended to improve the ability of organizations to deliver services. The charitable organizations at the top of the pyramid are likely to have most of the resources. Nine percent of the labour force is employed by these 78,000 charities and they may account for up to 13 percent of gross domestic product. But, half of them have revenues less than $50,000; 40 percent have revenues between $50,000 and half a million; 9 percent over $500,000; and just 2 percent have revenues over $5 million. If governments are interested in employing these organizations to deliver services or to substitute for government services, there are not many to choose from.

As I indicated at the outset, we have an opportunity to improve the ability of voluntary organizations to contribute both economically and socially to the quality of life in Canada. Governments give these organizations increased attention and some are attempting to develop initiatives to strengthen this set of institutions. In addition, public opinion would appear to be supportive of such initiatives. However, because of our lack of knowledge, we have little to guide our policy development and there is a need to lay the groundwork for more evidence-based policies. There is also a need for greater precision in the targeting of policy initiatives. The voluntary sector is extremely diverse and will be best served by policies that recognize this diversity. In the short term, the lack of clearly defined targets may be appropriate, given our lack of knowledge about the voluntary sector. However, in the longer term, there is a danger that opportunities to strengthen the voluntary sector may be missed.

PADDY BOWEN
Executive Director
Volunteer Canada

International Year of Volunteers and Government Responsibilities

The International Year of Volunteers (IYV) starts officially on 5 December 2000. Volunteer Canada has the lead on behalf of the voluntary sector working in partnership with Canadian Heritage and Human Resources Development Canada. I present here five general statements that reflect much of what has emerged in the other papers at a theoretical level, and will discuss our experiences with IYV against these general themes. It is very difficult to provide this kind of analysis and critique without the risk of offending people but there is a big difference between thinking about the individuals that one works with and how we work together and thinking about the way systems work. I have the highest regard for the individuals working on IYV but the system does not work well.

The first theme that I identified is that there is an integral, unavoidable tension between the experience of being a partner and of being in a funder-fundee relationship. So while for the International Year of Volunteers we are committed to joint decision-making, we still have contribution agreements that define and guide a linear relationship. *We* report to them. They do not report to us. With a number of new staff, Volunteer Canada is working with volunteer centres across the country. We have to detail what we are spending money on and who is doing what for the government. There are a lot of people at Heritage Canada and Human Resources Development Canada (HRDC) working on IYV but no one is reporting to us. We are not being told who is working, what they are doing, and what the output is. The jointness begins to be watered down as we deal with the realities of a contribution agreement-defined relationship.

On the other hand, the contribution-agreement relationship has proved to be a very effective way to move quickly, which we needed to do around IYV: For example, the development of a poster for IYV. There were some very interesting and rather tense discussions at one point on whether it would matter if Sheila Copps or, heaven forbid, the nine ministers in the reference group would like the poster or not. Were we going to have to get it signed off by them? In which case you can imagine we might get the poster for the next time we do the International Year of Volunteers in the world. I think it is slated for some time in the year 3000! So at that point we were able to waive the contribution agreement under everyone's nose and say, "Excuse me. You gave us the responsibility to develop a poster." Guess who gets the sign off? I do.

Another tension surfaces in terms of the relationship between a partner and a funder-fundee every time a new player comes into the game. There are many people in this room who have heard the rant: "IYV is not about making the federal government look good, it is about recognizing and celebrating the work of volunteers at the grassroots level." Well, one day there was some poor soul from the Privy Council Office (PCO) who stumbled into a meeting thinking he might be helpful. After receiving the rant, he left looking terribly shell-shocked, but there is a moral responsibility to do the rant. In fact, I have a little box that I carry with me because every time there is a new player we have to go back to beating them up and explaining the difference between being a partner and being a fundee.

And then finally, within this general area is the pervasive and lurking danger of ministerial interest. We are all fine. We can work things out between the bureaucrats and the voluntary sector until *the minister* starts to become excited. It is terrible. Actually what we want to do is bore the minister because then *she* won't care what we do. As soon as we start being good then the minister might be interested and, of course, if it suddenly occurrs to somebody that shaking the hand of a volunteer is almost as good as kissing a baby, we are in big trouble.

Now, alternatively, despite the aforementioned tensions, my second acknowledgement is that I believe that fundamentally the voluntary sector and government are interdependent. We serve the same citizens. And particularly on a issue like volunteerism we are jointly committed to the ideal of volunteerism, to its growth, its development, and its vitality in the voluntary sector particularly so that interdependence can be utilized by both parties to protect the voluntary sector. I will give you an example related to IYV. We made the federal government and the national organizations, specifically Volunteer Canada I think mostly has to bear responsibility for this, take a decision that no money from the national program is going out to the voluntary sector. The entire $6 million is coming to me. We could not (remembering Michael's pyramid) in any rational or fair way distribute dollars to the voluntary sector because, of course, the single defining characteristic of the whole sector is the involvement of volunteers. So, we could have cut everybody a cheque for $40 or we could invest the money in the development of resources and tools, such as social marketing messages that will ultimately strengthen the ability of the sector to engage volunteers and allow Canadians to feel good about themselves as volunteers. This was a potentially very difficult position for the federal government: to say publicly to the voluntary sector, "No. We are not giving you any money." But they are very nicely able to say now, "Blame them. That was Volunteer Canada's decision." And we likewise say, "Well look. We are working with them. What do you expect?" And so our interdependence has allowed us to move forward in what could have been a rather controversial way based on a kind of mutual decision-making.

My third observation is (and this is not going to be a surprise to anybody) that there is a real difference in being engaged in a process that is horizontal in nature versus one that deals with a single department and a single issue. The horizontality of the International Year of Volunteers program has been extremely challenging. Government itself, and this has been pointed out to me repeatedly by my colleagues in government, does not have good mechanisms to make decisions or work horizontally. Neither does the voluntary sector. We all deal in what we call "stove pipes." We have thought a lot of this through at the Voluntary Sector Roundtable and this creates real challenges for all of us. Promoting volunteerism is by definition a horizontal exercise. Volunteers appear in every part of the sector and, in fact, there are volunteers involved in 17 federal government departments, countless provincial departments as well as in paragovernmental organizations, the education system, etc. They are us. They are everywhere. So there is no way to do this in a non-horizontal fashion but we have been tripped up repeatedly by the challenges of horizontality.

Associated with this question of horizontality is one of the things that drives me crazy about the IYV process and is beginning to make me crazy in the Voluntary Sector Initiative (VSI) process. With respect, it is a rather untutored knee-jerk reaction on the part of my federal colleagues. I am referring to the government concern that it is dealing with the usual suspects, whether it is the Canadian Centre for Philanthropy, United Way, Community Foundations, NVO or Volunteer Canada, and that it should spread out and start talking to other people. Well, we five are national voluntary organizations, and I cannot really think of anyone else, except sometimes the Canadian Council on Social Development, that has our capacity and reach. But we have horizontal mandates within the voluntary sector and we are a very small number of organizations who do. So who else is going to lead on a horizontal initiative around volunteerism? I am tired of hearing that we need to go to other organizations. Would you want the Heart and Stroke Foundation to take the lead on volunteerism in Canada? There are some of us who, by virtue of our mandate, are going to be the usual suspects. The same is true down at the community level where we see local volunteer centres taking the lead and the same sort of accusations begin to fly. We need to be realistic, and following on what Michael Hall has said, understand how the voluntary sector is formulated and be prepared to work within that framework.

Another issue around horizontality that has been very interesting in terms of IYV has been the expectations. We are working with two lead departments, PCO and Treasury Board kind of circle us, and then we have Heritage Canada, HRDC, and Volunteer Canada. At the outset, it was certainly the expectation of the other departments that they would receive some sort of special status in terms of getting IYV money or resources. Our view, which I think shocked a lot of people, is that in this case we see Health or the Canadian International Development Agency (CIDA) or Department of the Environment no differently than we see voluntary organizations like Heart and Stroke and Boys and Girls Clubs, etc. If we are going to have a centralized program to develop resources and information, which is what we have decided, then that would also apply to other government departments, likewise to provincial governments. We convened a meeting of the provincial governments and said, "No. There isn't any money. There is no federal-provincial relationship. We have decided on a strategy and this applies to everybody." That was very, very surprising to other federal departments and has created a challenge.

My fourth observation is that there is a real difference in engaging in activities using a practice lens versus a policy lens. IYV first and foremost is about practice. My observation is that it is a very different kind of process when you get out of the policy treetops and down to the rank and file. One of our challenges in the sector is that people are not necessarily interested in or do not share in the kind of language and the fundamental approach that is required in thinking about policy. So what happens is that we, the sector, yank our colleagues out of the "doing" mode and ask them to think analytically about how the voluntary sector in Canada works. Tim Simboli mentioned this. He is in the middle of building and running a program and making sure that counsellors meet with clients, and then to suddenly pop in here is a little bit like finding yourself in wonderland. It is a very different kind of discourse. I observe this difference both inside the sector as well as when we work sector to government and I think we need to acknowledge that sometimes doers want to do and analysts want to analyze and we do not necessarily have to put the pressure on each other to be all things to all people. This extends to consultations. There is a kind of a political correctness to consultation and it worries me that through the Voluntary Sector Initiative we are going to consult the voluntary sector to death.

When looking at something like volunteerism (I don't want to oversimplify it except actually one of my best skills is oversimplifying), there is only so much you can do to enhance volunteering. We need to learn more about it. So we need to do some research on volunteering, not the voluntary sector, not the bigger stuff but around volunteering. We need to promote it to Canadians so we engaging in social marketing. We need Canadians to feel proud. They need to understand the scope and the impact of volunteering and we need to help organizations do a better job of volunteering and involving volunteers. This is now called capacity-building although it was not called that three years ago, and I do not know what it will be called two years from now. Basically it refers to helping us do a better job. Beyond that there is not that much else you can do to enhance volunteerism. It is both an extremely simple and an extremely complex process. It boils down to enhancing a relationship between that person who gives the time and passion and the organization that needs that time and passion. So it is my dear desire that we do not spend a whole lot of time and money going out and asking the sector over and over again, "What do you want us to do around volunteerism?" They are going to say, "Do some research, get some tools, do some social marketing." We heard the same thing over and over in the series of consultations prior to IYV. So once again it is part of my rant that we know what we are talking about, we know our sector, and there needs to be some trust to move ahead. This is going to play out in a lot of areas of the VSI. We need to be careful with consultations.

There is a final issue around the policy versus practice lens. One of the things we have not discussed here is that the advocacy process did not make it to a table through the VSI. Language can be fuzzy. So, for example, the federal government is extremely interested in having the voluntary sector participate in the policy debate. But we cannot do advocacy. And it is not 100 percent clear to a lot of us what the difference is. Is it tone of my voice that tells you if I am being an advocate versus a policy inputter, or is it whether I use swear words? I am not sure. We need to bring some clarity to those thoughts.

Finally, there are some cultural differences between the way the voluntary sector does things and the way government does things. I love watching meetings and we have had some great meetings where the bureaucrats all come in with that black book and all I have is some old scrap of paper.[2] Where's her book? I must not be serious if I don't have the book. All of the staff from Volunteer Canada come to the meeting, the receptionists, the volunteers, and they all pipe in but on the government side, the highest ranking person speaks

---

[2]It is common practice within the bureaucracy to keep notes in lined black books.

and everybody else nods and if that high ranking person leaves, then the next level begins to speak. I say, "Oh, you can talk." Within government there are set procedures and an established hierarchy for making decisions, while at Volunteer Canada it is pretty darn flat. This complicates the relationship.

I have decided that size matters, just the sheer size and scope of the government. For example, there is somebody at Heritage Canada who thinks full-time about logos and where they go on posters. It is wonderful because he knows everything about logos. But at Volunteer Canada, this is just such a tiny, tiny part of what we do. It is almost surreal since it is really a David and Goliath kind of thing. We just have to laugh. This brings me to my point that there is a difference even in style: the serious, earnest, sometimes humanless approach of a room full of bureaucrats compared to the institutionalized irreverence of the voluntary sector, particularly the part that I work in.

And finally, our attitudes to power are very different. Power in government comes from having money. Government plays the democratic legitimacy card and the voluntary sector plays the moral superiority card. We use political influence, charm, and popularity to get our way.

Finally, just a brief kind of wrap-up comment. IYV is one of the first joint initiatives out of the gate from the VSI and it proves to me that only when we do something together will we begin to explore both the limits and possibilities of working in partnership, and to understand what we mean and what we do not mean when we say we are going to be someone's partner. In the end, a lot of it does come down to the individuals involved and we are extremely lucky to be working with some of the best people in government on IYV. They are not only supportive and helpful, they let me give a speech like this and I do not think they will kill me!

MIYO YAMASHITA
Data Security Officer
Mount Sinai Hospital

Privacy Issues in the Third Sector

Why privacy? Because quite simply surveillance is pervasive. Let me share a couple of examples with you. The average Canadian over the age of 18 is currently listed in over 18,000 databases, many of which are contained in organizations in the third sector such as schools and hospitals. In the United States it is possible to purchase online information about your neighbour's speeding tickets, child-support payments, or bounced cheques and some US medical Web sites will sell you a complete list of your neighbour's urinary tract infections for just $9.00.

Finally, your own computer might even be spying on you! I do not want to sound paranoid but I will share a story with you. Last Christmas a software developer in Massachusetts named Richard Smith downloaded a program from the Internet called Z Bubbles. Z Bubbles is designed to help you with your online shopping. It is manufactured by a subsidiary of Amazon called Alexa and when you log on to an e-commerce site, it provides you with information about products and it also points you to similar products online that might be available at cheaper prices. In order to do this, Z Bubbles has to collect certain personal information about you and send it back to Alexa. It has to know, for example, the kinds of Web sites that you are going to and the types of products and services that you might be interested in purchasing. But it also does something a little more sinister than that. It actually monitors your online activities even when you are *not* shopping and reports them back to Alexa. For instance, Mr. Smith discovered that when he went to an airline Web site to check on his daughter's plane reservation that Z Bubbles was sending information back to Alexa containing his daughter's name, her age (she was 14), her address, her flight numbers, and even her dietary restrictions for her meals on those flights. Furthermore, Mr. Smith also discovered that Z Bubbles was sending other information back to Alexa, including his name, address, credit card number and the titles of several DVDs that he was considering purchasing on a Web site called buy.com.

When I heard this story, I decided to call Alexa myself to verify their privacy policy. They told me that I had nothing to worry about — that at the present time Alexa has no interest in correlating any of the information they collect on customers with their individual accounts, but that in future their privacy policy could be subject to change without notice. Furthermore, they also admitted that if Alexa were ever sold, their customers' information could be sold along with the company as part of its assets.

So, privacy is important because surveillance is pervasive. Let me explain what I mean when I talk about surveillance and then I will comment on some of its implications and issues you need to consider in your work in the third sector. When I talk about "surveillance" I am using this term very broadly. In the past, surveillance has been used to refer to specific activities usually having to do with policing and espionage, but I am using it here as a shorthand term to cover the many and expanding range of activities within which your personal information is collected. Sometimes this happens in the third sector, for example, when you go to a hospital as a patient. By law, you have to give up certain information about yourself, both clinical and demographic.

But increasingly, however, surveillance is also occuring in the commercial sector and this has specific implications for this sector. All this collected information is described by a British sociologist, Roger Clark, as your "data persona." Increasingly, in the twenty-first century we are becoming known to organizations by our data persona. So, for example, rather than being known in an organization by your name or by the unique qualities of your character/ personality, you are known by a number, an address, a postal code — which contains valuable information about your socio-economic status — by the kind of car you drive, the kind of house you live in, by the number of children you have, by the number of pets you own, and, even, by the kind of pet food these animals consume. In fact, Roger Clark has estimated that the level of detail contained in the average data persona has increased by about 150 percent since organizations started constructing detailed consumer profiles over a decade ago.

The surveillance construction of consumer profiles — or client or data profiles if you work in the third sector — is experienced with ambivalence and indeed can have some positive, concrete advantages. For example, modern surveillance systems are meant to ensure that you are paid correctly and on time, that you receive the appropriate welfare benefits, that you can drive on an electronic toll highway, that you can receive the latest news about various consumer products, that you can purchase goods with credit cards instead of the more cumbersome cash, that you can purchase products online, etc. This might explain the lack of resistance to surveillance in any formalized sense. In addition, it is important to note that contemporary surveillance is more subtle now than its predecessor. Surveillance cameras are being replaced by global positioning satellites. Passwords are being replaced by seamless, biometric, authentication techniques such as voiceprints or retinal scans. And I already talked about software like Z Bubbles, which, because of its electronic character can collect information and send it back to Alexa without you even knowing about it.

In addition, surveillance is expanding quickly, often as a result of processes intended to pursue goals like efficiency and productivity. So, for example, one day your health card may be replaced by a smart card that houses your medical data and prescription history. Every time you go to visit a doctor or hospital, this card will be swiped. Information about you could eventually be sent to the Ministry of Health, other care providers, hospital foundations and researchers. Similarly, a lot of smart cards are being used at universities in the US. They contain everything from the courses a student is enrolled in to parking privileges, to the library books he or she borrows, to the kind of food purchased at the campus cafeteria. The problem with these kinds of things is that while they offer definite advantages such as convenience, they also pose the problem of function "creep," where information collected on the card for one purpose is used for another purpose without the knowledge or consent of the data subject.

So what does this mean for the third sector? I am going to talk in very general terms. I argue that privacy and surveillance have four implications for the third sector.

The first has to do with public opinion. In a nutshell, consumers are becoming increasingly aware of contemporary surveillance practices and that means they are demanding greater accountability from *all* organizations. For example, a 1995 survey by the Public Interest Advocacy Centre found 76 percent of Canadians feel that they have less control over their personal information than they did ten years ago. The same survey also found that, increasingly, Canadians are demanding that their permission be sought before their information is either shared with another organization or used for a purpose other than that for which it was originally collected. So, as an organization, you need to remember that the Canadian public is demanding increasing accountability from you about how you handle their personal information.

The second factor that you have to consider in your work in the third sector has to do with new legislative initiatives. Most privacy laws as they currently stand regulate the collection, use and disclosure of personal information held by government bodies. That is going to change, at least at the federal level, beginning in January 2001 with the *Personal Information Protection and Electronic Documents Act*, otherwise known as the former Bill C-6. It is based on a set of ten fair information-handling principles developed by the Canadian Standards Association. In Ontario, we will probably be subject to a broad Privacy Act that will be based on the same set of fair information-handling principles and will necessarily apply to charitable organizations.

The fair information principles were developed in the 1980s by the Organisation for Economic Co-operation and Development, and form the basis of many privacy laws in the western world. To become compliant with the new privacy laws, you need to review your daily information-handling practices and make sure that you are compliant with each of the ten principles. So, for example, you might want to think about designating or hiring a person who is responsible for how you use information in your organization in order to satisfy the "accountability" principle. Similarly, to satisfy the "minimum data collection" principle, you need to make sure that every piece of personal information you collect has an identified purpose, and that that purpose is legitimate. You might also have to obtain the consent of individuals in order to use their information in certain ways. So, for example, at hospitals where I am currently working, we cannot pass on information to our hospital foundation without asking for permission first from our patients. Finally, it is also important to note that depending on the kind of information you have, you will need to implement appropriate security safeguards to protect the sensitivity of that information (e.g., firewalls, passwords, VPNs[3]).

Third, and finally, you have to think about the watchdog and educational roles that third sector organizations have traditionally played. I believe that it is the responsibility of all educational institutions to educate students about contemporary surveillance practices, to engage students in open, critical, imaginative dialogue about these practices and where appropriate provide information on new social theories of surveillance. As third sector organizations, there are advocacy roles you may be expected to play in the traditions, for example, of the Electronic Privacy Information Center in Washington and Electronic Frontier Canada. These organizations do everything from developing online petitions, to participating in public anti-surveillance demonstrations, to publishing various newspaper articles to increase public awareness about privacy.

In summary, contemporary surveillance systems are marked by three features. They are institutionally central, they are increasingly subtle (Z Bubbles), and they have expanded into new areas, most notably, the commercial sector. As a result, the third sector needs to consider three privacy issues: growing public awareness about privacy, and growing accountability for third sector organizations as a result; new privacy laws that will affect how you handle personal information; and new advocacy and educational roles for certain third sector organizations.

Further works in this area are by Roger Clark who wrote about the data persona; Oscar Gandy; Anthony Giddens; David Lyon, a sociologist at Queen's; Gary Marx who talks about surveillance and policing; and Priscilla Regan who

---

[3]Virtual private networks.

talks about US privacy policy.[4] And there are also various anti-surveillance activities to become involved in through some of the privacy organizations I mentioned earlier.

Finally, I conclude with something I share with my clients when I help them design corporate data security programs. I tell them, "However you feel about privacy, please take it seriously and don't treat it like another boring, bureaucratic item on your already very long list of things to do." As educators, as lawyers, as students with bright critical minds and most importantly, as consumers and as citizens who are subject to contemporary surveillance practices everyday, you have both a responsibility and the means to counter these practices and to protect your personal privacy and autonomy.

DAVID CAMERON
Professor of Political Science
University of Toronto

Patterns of Associations: Managing Linguistic Differences

"Patterns of Linguistic Association in Voluntary Organizations" is the research project that we have been running for the last two years, and is in the final stages. This will be a preliminary reporting of that project.

In response to the question: "What is Pierre Trudeau's greatest contribution?" I would answer, not the Charter of Rights and Freedoms and the patriation

---

[4]Roger Clarke, "The Digital Persona and Its Application to Data Surveillance," *Information Society* 10 (1994); Oscar Gandy, *The Panoptic Sort: A Political Economy of Personal Information* (Boulder: Westview, 1993); Anthony Giddens, *Modernity and Self-Identity: Self and Society in the Late Modern Age* (Stanford: Stanford University Press, 1991); David Lyon, *Surveillance Society: Monitoring Everyday Life* (Philadelphia: Open University, 2001); Gary Marx, *Undercover: Police Surveillance in America* (Berkeley: University of California Press, 1988); Gary Marx and Cyrille Fijnaut (eds.), *Undercover: Police Surveillance in Comparative Perspective* (Boston: Kluwer, 1995); Reginald Whitaker, *The End of Privacy: How Total Surveillance Is Becoming a Reality* (New York: New Press, 1999).

of the constitution, the conventional answer, but in fact the passage of the *Official Languages Act* in 1969. It represents a transformative change in the way that Canadians over time came to understand their society, particularly English-speaking Canadians. I think that what it offered was the essential minimum to francophones in this country so far as the character of the federal government and the definition of the country was concerned. But in English-speaking Canada, over the last 30 years or so, it has had a transformative effect and our research project examines some of the effects of that period in our lives.

The question the project asked related to language and language practice in civil society. We had observed that the literature on language at the level of politics and public life was indeed copious. But this project involves a larger question about the redefinition of our country and of the meaning of citizenship in our country. It addresses what has been happening not at the governmental level but elsewhere in our community. What changes are being experienced? What practices are being altered? We know something about this with respect to educational practices, second language education, immersion programs, and so on. But in the ongoing lives of citizens, what is happening? So we asked the question, "what impact have these questions of language had on civil society?" We decided that we would look at a selection of voluntary organizations and chart their experience and their life linguistically over the last 30 years or so. We did that because there really was very little research on it. The major piece of work in this area goes back to a very good and interesting study by John Meisel of Queen's University and Vincent Lemieux, a political scientist at Laval, who did a piece of research for the Royal Commission on Bilingualism and Biculturalism in the 1960s. And since then, there has been effectively nothing.

We decided that we would extend their approach. They had used a case study approach, for good reasons. And we did the same thing. We decided that what we would do is to try and replicate some of the studies and cases that they had examined in the 1960s but add some others as well, some that would relate to new political movements and organizations, issues that have arisen since their study. And we would look at these associations over time from the 1960s on. Thus, we were really charting the life histories of these associations over the last 30 years or so to try to get a fix on how they encountered the language issue and how they responded to it. Were there certain moments of major crisis? What happened if there were? If there were not, why not? Was it management by neglect or very astute, hands-on management of the issue? In general, we aimed to understand what had happened linguistically in these organizations.

The funding for this was an absolute nightmare. We had aspired to do about 16 or more cases. We ended up with 11 case studies in the following areas. In each case, we asked a researcher, an academic, in many cases someone who had worked in the area on other matters, to apply his or her talents and experience to the particular case study. Bill Coleman from McMaster University looked at business associations. Don Stevenson and Richard Gilbert from Toronto looked at municipal organizations. Jane Jenson, one of my project co-directors looked at the Canadian Council for Social Development. Richard Simeon from the University of Toronto, the second co-director, looked at the Heart and Stroke Foundation. Others looked at the Canadian Jewish Congress, sports associations, the Gay and Lesbian Organization, WUSC, Amnesty International, the Canadian Medical Association and agriculture.

We laid out a general approach that each would use so that when we come to the reporting stage, we could tease out the findings, making some comparisons among the experiences of the different associations. Willingly, happily and perhaps unusually for academics, most of them actually did follow the approach in the way that we had hoped they would. As a result, we have a collection of very good empirical examinations of the French-English issue with respect to these associations. I will summarize some general findings, but unfortunately not in great detail.

The first point goes back to Trudeau and the *Official Languages Act.* There has clearly been an institutionalization of the language issue, if these groups are any indication of the organizations that have pretensions to standing at the Canadian level. It looks as if it is difficult if not impossible to assert yourself as a Canadian organization, particularly at the level of the country as a whole, and not address the language question. You may fail, you may succeed and you may do it elegantly or partially. You may have problems but you cannot ignore it. This represents significant social change, an attitudinal change in every organization. It was a matter that the organization felt it necessary to address.

The second finding is that there has been quite a lot of progress. We did not know what we would encounter. There was an open question because we had heard many stories of problems in the various organizations. We did not have a real sense of whether things were reasonably healthy or the reverse. We realize that 11 organizations is a small sample of the sector, but on the basis of that sample, we feel that a good deal of positive progress has been made. In fact, several of the organizations had more difficulty and more tension in their operation and policy-making in the 1960s and early seventies than there seemed to be in the 1990s. In a way, that should not be surprising, given that the assertion of French as a national tongue, as a Canadian official language, was a challenge that was being put to Canadian society in a way that it had not been before.

Another finding was that civil society is ambiguous or more elusive than expected. Michael Hall discussed how we have different meanings and different terms and that we are not always as conscious of this as we should be. But we used civil society as defined in the literature as face-to-face encounters and neighbourhood networks of contacts. It is a fairly immediate citizenship-based experience. That is not, in fact, what we found in the associations we examined. We have in the associational world the equivalent of the elite accommodation model that is found in the political world. In other words, the association that crossed language groups was the association at the level of leadership. There were no reports about extensive direct exchanges, encounters, and connections across the language cultures at the level of the membership itself. Staff operate the associations. The senior elected leadership establish how they encounter and work with one another and work with government in the interested areas. It was that band at the upper level where the linguistic accommodation was really working. Part of what has been going on in this country has been a kind of a continuing project of definition of two linguistic communities where one can live a fairly full and rich and complete life within the framework of one or the other of these communities. That mode of co-existence was reflected in our findings on associations.

Perhaps not surprisingly, a variety of organizational arrangements were found. These included separation and sovereignty association and alliances and confederation and federal relationships and units in reform. All are in evidence in the associations. It speaks to the extraordinary creativity of the people involved; what is more, they are not constrained by politics, they are not often in the public eye. They are simply trying to make something work for themselves and their membership. Thus, they have experimented and done what they wanted, whatever they can. This means that there is a great deal of creativity and variety in the way in which associations have organized themselves. In some cases, there is a kind of split sovereignty association model, for example, at Amnesty International where their Quebec francophone branch was created. If you ask about the relationships now between those two, they are excellent. They both tend to concentrate on different parts of the world in their activities, cooperating as necessary, but they function as two different organizations. In contrast, in the agricultural field, partially because of the strength of the Quebec agricultural industry and the sheer heft of that community in national agricultural matters, there is a form of federal arrangement with a very impressive insistence on full-scale, linguistic equality at the associational federal level. There is a wonderful array of different experiments and arrangements in the various associations.

In my own research on this project, I have found that there is a sense that the *Official Languages Act* and Bill 101 map the associations being examined. In other words, there will be an association at the Canadian level in which there are two languages that get expressed more or less, but almost invariably with the tilt to English. A francophone functioning at the Canadian level will carry the heavier burden of conducting the business and dealing with the language question. But often organizations have gone some distance to recognizing the notion that there are two official languages that should be addressed and treated on the basis of equality. The Quebec wing of the association or federation will then be modelled within the framework of Bill 101, meaning essentially a French-language operation that is more or less accepted by the participants.

A variety of factors explain the different experiences and trajectories of these associations. Clearly, the socio-political context is one. The *Official Languages Act* has set a policy context, a broad political context to which many organizations have responded. There are many kinds of associations from many different sectors with many different mandates. I have mentioned the role of the Quebec agricultural community as an example in which the strength of that sector is one of the dominant determinants of full-scale recognition of the two languages in the federation. And then you have a range of internal factors: the membership base, the organizational structure, the leadership, the resources available. All of those go into making up the ultimate outcome. One thing that became clear is that in many of these organizations leadership is crucial. A single person who is relatively strong and active and *in situ* long enough, can have a major impact in advancing or retarding a situation such as addressing the linguistic questions that these organizations face.

SELECTED COMMENTS FROM THE DISCUSSION

SAGA WILLIAMS
Health Policy Analyst
Anishinabek Health Commission
Union of Ontario Indians

I have two questions. David, when you looked at the patterns of associations managing linguistic differences, did you look exclusively at English-French, or did you look at the reality of indigenous languages, how they did not receive equal respect in relation to that whole development of a two-language country, and what that meant for regional areas located in the backyard of various large, indigenous people's reservations or communities?

DAVID CAMERON

The short answer is that we focused exclusively on French and English and there were considerations like whether regions would explain different difficulties or crises that organizations might face or other factors. Where they came up we included them in the equation as explanatory factors but our centre of research interest was French and English.

SAGA WILLIAMS

My other question is for Ms. Yamashita. You did mention in passing, collecting information on, for example, health care and specifically you spoke of HIV and AIDS. I know that in working with other volunteer coordinators in HIV and AIDS there is a lot of data being collected. You need a database in order to call up your volunteers as quickly as possible. Some of us are privileged and some of us are not. But the question is, how do we in the voluntary sector make sure that we are putting together databases that do not leave us open to Internet breaches or misuse? Are there any processes that can be imbedded into either board decision-making or actual organizational structures to safeguard ourselves? We have two databases, one for volunteers and one for HIV patients. The support department keeps one, the volunteer department keeps the other. We make all efforts to ensure they do not cross.

MIYO YAMASHITA

You probably want to approach this from two angles. One is a policy angle and the other is a technology angle. Bear in mind that under new privacy laws, the Office of the Information and Privacy Commissioner will have broad powers of investigation, including the ability to come into your organization and require that you change your information management practices as well as the right to assign fines which are relatively stiff and to publicize their findings. To avoid any exposure to them from a policy angle you want to make sure you have access policies around your databases that outline the information contained in those databases, the uses for that information, who has access to that information, and under what circumstances. From a technology end it is a little more complicated depending on how those databases are linked. For example, if they are linked with other organizations, other volunteer groups, then you have to consider more security, including a virtual private network or a firewall and that depends on the kinds of technologies you have in place. Once these new laws come into effect, you should be able to get some advice from the actual Office of the Information and Privacy Commissioner.

PADDY BOWEN

I have a quick comment regarding the policy around privacy. Notwithstanding our concerns around privacy, it does not let any organization off the hook in terms of appropriately screening volunteers, and collecting information that is necessary for making the decisions around proper allocation of people to jobs based on the duty of care. You need to protect your clientele.

JOHN SAXBY
Canadian International Development Agency
Canadian Partnerships Branch

I would like to make an observation that was triggered by some of the remarks by Paddy and Michael. It has to do with the question of the capacity of the voluntary sector to intervene in the policy dialogue. It is important not to confuse a lack of power with an apparent lack of capacity. I have been part of lots of initiatives by voluntary sector organizations which have been well prepared and well researched and well presented but which have gone absolutely nowhere simply because of lack of political, or economic or other kinds of leverage. In a lot of the discussion that goes on, because capacity is a technical word or it is used that way a lot of the time, it is easier to assign problems and unevenness and burrs beneath the saddle in the so-called policy dialogue to problems of capacity on the part of the sector or organizations within the sector when what is really at issue are substantial discrepancies in the power and privileged interests.

MICHAEL HALL

I agree with John about the importance of not confusing capacity and power. I would just suggest that capacity is a necessary condition to engage in these dialogues. It is not sufficient to ensure that you will have the effect that you want and that is the power you mention. I agree that we should not confuse them, but do not underestimate the need to pay attention to capacity.

MARILYN HAY
Human Resources Development Canada

Some of Paddy's comments about the role of the national organization versus some of the local levels were reminiscent of discussions we have inside the federal government. I stress that there is value for any number of reasons in getting people involved and engaged across the board, while recognizing capacity and time and constraint issues. It gives a sense of ownership, of being able to see oneself in this process, of having a voice and all of that. We often find that we do have things to contribute within the federal sector, for example, in the policy debate from a local or an operational level.

PADDY BOWEN

Yes, people need to participate at all levels, but they need the support and the capacity and sometimes maybe an intermediary. When the Broadbent Panel listened to the issues on accountability, a fair amount of time had to be spent explaining to people what the question was, how to make them understand what they were being asked to agree to.

MARILYN HAY

In terms of the privacy issues, the horse is gone and you are trying to slam the barn door and there are 18,000 different corrals already. I sometimes wonder if we shouldn't grapple and debate a whole lot more with our whole concepts and issues around privacy. Sometimes I think we are schooled by the fact that we grew up reading George Orwell's *1984* which has made us paranoid about who has information on us. This is not to say that there are not predators out there and that we need to know how to deal with them, but sometimes we might be better off if we stopped thinking about who the predators are and examined how the information being collected is being used. Whatever rules and processes we have in Canada will not protect us completely. Access and privacy laws are extremely expensive, and we are spending more time and resources responding to inquiries than we do delivering our services. We should have a real debate about what privacy and surveillance mean in a global sense.

MIYO YAMASHITA

I have two quick comments about privacy to respond to your remarks. The first thing that has to be said about privacy laws is that they are expensive to implement and there is no way around it. As a privacy scholar I would say it is more expensive to not have the laws. Once you have certain surveillance systems in place, it is extremely difficult to alter them or have them removed. I should also point out that historically the development of privacy legislation in Canada stems from European privacy laws, mainly the European Union Data Protection directive that came into effect in 1998. This directive contains transporter data flow clauses which state that if any country in the European Union (EU) wants to share information with a country or a company or an organization outside the EU, they must ensure that comparable, adequate safeguards are in place. Hence, the development of Bill C-6 in Canada.

The second is that privacy has some real business advantages and that a lot of proponents for these laws are not paranoid security buffs but businesses. For example, the Canadian Direct Marketers Association and the Canadian Bankers Association both lobbied for Bill C-6 because they felt there needed to be privacy rules in place in order to support e-commerce initiatives. Business sees these initiatives as a small cost in the larger scheme of things.

KEITH BANTING
School of Policy Studies
Queen's University

Paddy and Michael, would you comment on the level of volunteerism in the last couple of decades given the fact that the participation in the labour force has changed radically or perhaps that change is offset by the fact that there has been a great deal of downsizing in the last few years?

MICHAEL HALL

We know how the level of volunteerism has changed since 1987 as there have been two studies. Over a ten-year period, it increased, primarily among the youth. There has been an increase in the participation rate. People are volunteering less time, however, but because there has been an increase in the participation rate, the actual number of hours has increased. Most of that increase is happening among the youth and appears to be job-related, trying to get entry into the job market.

PADDY BOWEN

Michael has given you a thumbnail sketch. We have great numbers around volunteerism, and especially around the International Year of Volunteers and the National Volunteerism Initiative. We are very concerned that we move in lock step as we increase awareness and call for more Canadians to volunteer and to be able to contribute meaningfully. At the same time, we have to invest in the capacity of organizations to involve those volunteers meaningfully. We need research on this aspect of capacity. There is some evidence that it is getting harder for organizations to consider things like screening and privacy and volunteer management. We all know that the volunteer manager is the first person to go when there are cuts. So we push back very hard on jurisdictions that would like to beat the drums and get more volunteers without the simultaneous investment in organizational capacity.

CONCLUSION

FUTURE TRENDS IN PUBLIC POLICY AND THE THIRD SECTOR .

The Honourable Jenny Kwan, Minister of Community Development, Co-operatives and Volunteers for the Government of British Columbia concluded the conference with her reflections on the evolving relationship between the voluntary sector and governments in Canada. While the new relationship raises questions and creates challenges for policymakers, it is vital to the growth of the nation. While building a partnership between governments and voluntary organizations are important at the policy and sectoral levels, community engagement and individual participation is important at the grassroots level. Significant activity and growth at both levels is essential to ensuring a healthy and vibrant polity where citizens both give and are well served.

JENNY KWAN
Minister
Community Development, Cooperatives and Volunteers
Government of British Columbia

The evolving partnership between government and the voluntary sector continues to raise questions and I think create new challenges for policymakers as well as the community at large.

To understand the current, complex relationships between all levels of government and the third sector we need to reflect on how it has been affected by economic trends of the past 30 or 40 years. A short decade ago governments started expanding social programs and taking on more responsibility to care for individuals and families. This meant that the roles that were traditionally performed by members of the community — particularly women — were actually being filled over time by professionals. Before long, people became accustomed to and depended upon a new and organized system of social services. Then faced with falling revenues, escalating debt payments in the mid-1980s, all levels of government began cutting the social programs that people had come to depend on. And as many participants have said, the third sector became more important than ever before to the social fabric of the Canadian communities. Twenty years ago who would have guessed that in the year 2000, we would have thousands of Canadians in cities whose lives would be impacted by things like mental illness, substance misuse, the drug challenges, childhood traumas, and violence facing women. Or that at the core of every urban area would be countless men, women, and children without adequate housing and in many cases, without any home at all? Who would have guessed that we would have sexual assault centres and food banks everywhere? And who could have predicted that these services, so essential to the most vulnerable members of our society, would be primarily staffed by volunteers?

This raises several important questions about the current relationship between government and the third sector. Should we expect volunteer organizations to carry on the responsibility of addressing the social needs of our communities? Is it government's role to assume this responsibility despite the issues of cost, lack of effectiveness and inefficiencies that people often complain characterize many government programs? Or is the answer somewhere in between — resting in a new and dynamic balance in which government and the third sector can work more closely together to find innovative, cost-efficient ways of delivering services that are essential in Canadian communities?

Great Britain's prime minister, Tony Blair, addressed this very important issue in a recent speech. He said:

> In the first half of this century, we learned that the community cannot achieve its aims without the help of government providing essential services, and a backdrop of security. In the second half of the century we learned that government cannot achieve its aims without the energy and commitment of others.... So government and community need each other. They need to act in tandem ... And history shows that most successful societies are those that harness the energies of volunteer action, giving due recognition to the third sector of voluntary and community organizations.

If Tony Blair is correct, and I think he is, the best way to build a healthy society is for government to work with volunteer organizations, to provide for the practical support they need to help people in their communities. I will talk more about how the Canadian governments are approaching that subject below.

Twenty years ago, governments in western society tended to take the voluntary sector for granted. Volunteers were found everywhere there was a need for selflessness and generosity of spirit. They came, as volunteers always have, from all strata of society, all ethnic groups, all ages and all abilities. Women were simply expected to provide volunteer service in their community, whether as part of a volunteer organization or simply by being neighbourly. For the wives of many community leaders, for few of the leaders themselves were women, lending their name to a worthy cause was part of their "job description." Women were expected to do volunteer work and that is what they did. Today, the work of volunteers has become, in many cases, more complex, more organized, and more widespread. And even in the developed world, their work has become integral to the social fabric that makes us a civil society. In some parts of the world, like the sub-Sahara region of Africa where nations have been ravaged by warfare and HIV/AIDS, volunteers provide the only social safety net for people and the victims. It is the volunteers who ensure children in the communities have enough to eat, clothes to wear, and the chance to attend school. They accomplish this through countless hours of unpaid work and by donating what little they can spare from their own meagre incomes.

If we look at volunteerism in its most basic terms, we can see it as a connection between individuals. One person reaches out to help another who responds and in the exchange they both find a sense of belonging. In the words of the United Nations, in literature describing the year 2001 as the International Year of Volunteers,

> All volunteer service is based on an act of will of an individual. She or he can decide to seek to be of help to others or not to be. Every great movement in human history has begun with such an act of will on the part of one or more individuals. While there is progress in every society, many other individuals and groups suffer poverty, disability, oppression, a deteriorating environment.

The International Year of Volunteers (2001) will not be the success intended unless there is lasting change, a legacy for the future, that builds on strong partnerships between sectors to manage and support the millions of volunteers who give their time, energy, resources and compassion, whatever their cause. Volunteering creates a sense of belonging. A sense of belonging creates community. And community, the very basis of what we know as civil society, creates the building blocks of our province, our country, and around the globe. We can surely say that fostering and supporting volunteerism promotes connectedness and through that community development.

Politicians in governments, especially at the provincial and national levels, are unaccustomed to relating to and legislating for a unit as loosely defined as a community. This is because, of course, a community does not necessarily have a geographic area. It can be any grouping of people with mutual interests or a common focus. For example, all the people who are volunteering their time in British Columbia to save the Vancouver Island Marmot, a cute and nearly extinct animal that looks like a cross between a groundhog and a gopher, can be considered part of a community, even though they may live in different geographic locations.

In British Columbia we are currently considering ways to give communities tools to achieve greater equity as a means of achieving economic and social sustainability. We are looking at doing this by giving them more authority and control over their natural resources and development plans. We want to find ways to build on the expertise and resources that communities already have, but we often hear from people that the greatest strengths are in fact the people and the talents that are there. And the question is, how can government help and what can we do to ensure that we draw on those talents voluntarily or otherwise?

In looking for ways to identify new partnerships with communities to address local needs, we are consulting, although not to the point of exhaustion, with many community partners, including the voluntary sector, to establish what a regional and community development act might look like. This act can potentially rebalance the existing imbalance of power between government and the community. Concerns and fears that I often hear with respect to the structure of partnership centre around the question of government's willingness to give up power and control, and act in the manner they say that they would like: to invest and to believe in the community itself and the communities that put forward countless hours of dedication and commitment to volunteer work.

Much of the community development work we are engaged in involves building the capacity of a geographic area to diversify its economic base, to regenerate and to move on after a major employer, such as a mill or a mine, shuts down. Or, as in the case of the Downtown Eastside of Vancouver — the area often called the "poorest postal code in all of Canada" — we are trying to revitalize an inner city area that has a complex web of issues including substance misuse. This small area has the highest rate of HIV/AIDS infection in

North America and some of the worst housing conditions one could ever imagine. The Downtown Eastside may not feel like a community to outsiders passing through, yet it is a strong activist and dedicated community. About six years ago, the community finally managed to get the local government to recognize them as a neighbourhood, to finally get the name of the Downtown Eastside on the local maps to say "This is a community of residents, of small business people, and people who deserve not to be judged by the outside but valued for the strength that they bring to the table."

This work is done by the volunteers, the organizations, the people who are critical to the survival of this community. They are a source of continued hope and a source of inspiration. It is the oldest area in the city and the second-most stable neighbourhood in spite of its challenges. It is near the water and ideal for high-priced condominiums that traditionally displace low-income residents into even worse conditions. It is constantly under the threat of gentrification. Largely through the grassroots effort of activists and volunteers, most of them residents of the area, the Downtown Eastside has become recognized as legitimate and everyone within it is legitimate as well. The volunteers in this dynamic area have become a showcase of volunteerism and activism. Through their efforts they have been successful in bringing about one of the most used libraries with the highest numbers of volunteers in British Columbia, if not in all of Canada. They have been able to establish the Four Corners Community Savings, bringing banking services to a community that had not been able to access them previously, and hosting operas for local residents, and street programs for drug users to showcase their talents. Their volunteerism included strong advocacy for social change and they have highlighted the plight of Downtown Eastside residents to the local, provincial, and national governments. They have worked tirelessly with all three levels of government for solutions to the complex social needs in the area while continuing to deliver services to those in need. Some of these volunteers have themselves recovered from difficult lives involving drug addiction or prostitution. And they are living proof that society gains when all people are treated with dignity and respect and given opportunities and choices. But there needs to be a balance between volunteer work, activism and, of course, political will. This is where government needs to focus its attention.

On the other side, some of our neighbourhoods adjacent to the Downtown Eastside have shown that they are frustrated, if not outright hostile, toward some of the innovative solutions that have been brought about by the activists in the community. They have called on all three levels of government to end the provision of social support or services to the drug-addicted population.

They have marched in the streets and have collected thousands of signatures and petitions against the residents of the Downtown Eastside.

This raises more difficult questions such as:

- What is the role of government as it tries to ensure all community members gain legitimacy and a sense of belonging when some feel that this group of individuals is undeserving and cannot possibly contribute or be contributing members to our society, and just wish that they would go away?
- How can government give communities an appetite for embracing risk when they want it to happen anywhere but in their own back yard?
- How do we work toward changing people's attitudes?
- In a democratic civil society, should the powerful and the strong have the right to overshadow and define which members of our society have the right to participate fully?

To me, the answer is obvious. Governments are called on to provide leadership, but I want to share that leadership role with the community and especially with those who believe in the concept of civil society. It is in that joint partnership where we can build the political power to move and make changes. In that instance, size does not necessarily mean that it is better. Small can be loud and it can be strong and you can build on that size and duplicate that strength.

As has been discussed, the volunteer sector enjoys a high level of public trust. Indeed, 70 to 80 percent of people think that the third sector do the job better and that it can be trusted to do the job better than government. Perhaps this is because volunteerism is based on the natural human instinct to help others and that is seen as a social rather than as an economic exchange, an exchange between the benefactor and the beneficiary. But even the highly trusted volunteer sector must operate in an increasingly distrustful and litigious world. Some well-established volunteer organizations, widely believed to be contributing to civil societies have been financially ruined by court judgements that require them to pay millions of dollars in damages. In fact, the issue of liability for board members, for the financial affairs of a volunteer organization and the conduct of its members may need to be resolved through legislation. Good people who are legitimately concerned about carrying the financial health of a volunteer organization on their backs are refusing to become board members. Others know that the potential risks are high and they are still prepared to serve. Is it reasonable in a civil society that these citizens should have to put themselves and their families at personal financial risk? The situation is challenging and complex and many difficulties can arise when government attempts to legislate for the volunteer sector. In this case, for example, if we create legislation to protect the board members we could limit or take away the rights of the potential victims. This issue is critical and will affect the nature of the third sector significantly. BC has agreed to lead the work in this area with our national, provincial, and territorial partners.

I believe that government should increase practical support to the volunteer sector as a way to strengthen our communities and to improve the quality of life for our residents. In general, the BC government allows for two types of public support for the volunteer sector. First, it provides short-term assistance to empower an organization and to build capacity. The second is less specific and involves the ongoing funding that is often given to large organizations that work with government to achieve a common goal. The first, short-term or project funding, allows government to direct scarce resources to clearly defined and targeted results and outcomes. This way, through the work of volunteers, government can put patches on the safety net without raising taxes while balancing the budget, a demand that has become a mantra for many Canadians.

When government provides funds to volunteer organizations the normal procedure is for the organizations to apply for the project funding and for public servants to decide which organizations and projects would receive government funds. But is it fair for public servants to decide who should get funded and how much? Should government only fund projects consistent with government policies? What about projects a particular government does not agree with or agencies that seem dedicated to advocating against the government? Earlier there was discussion about the importance of considering new models for decision-making. In British Columbia we have begun to change our evaluation process so that government employees are not the only ones deciding which volunteer projects receive government funding. In the InVOLveBC program the Ministry of Community Development, Cooperatives and Volunteers' voluntary organization support program, a 23-person panel including 12 members of the voluntary sector, has just finished evaluating this round of funding applications. This means that the third sector itself has the deciding voice in who would receive the $1 million contributions from government.

This leads to another issue: institutionalization in the volunteer sector. The words "volunteer bureaucracy" seem contradictory at first glance but the larger an organization becomes, the more costly it becomes to administer. Large volunteer organizations develop an elaborate infrastructure of chapters, networks, fundraisers, professionals, committees and annual meetings and even conferences, all characteristics of a bureaucracy. How do volunteer organizations expand without becoming bureaucratic? Is government's role to help small, grassroots-oriented organizations develop and build capacity? If so, how do we ensure accountability and sound investment of taxpayers' money given that the small organizations tend not to have the proven track record of the large organization? And yet, in my own personal bias, those are the organizations perhaps with the better capacity to reach out to people. What risk factors are government and community members willing to accept with respect to investing in smaller community groups that really need help to build community capacity? To top it all off, what about the element of advocacy? Activist volunteer organizations often have a political message to send. Social change does not take place in a non-political vacuum. Should government support advocacy work that has political implications?

For government to facilitate this work it brings us back to the fundamental question of funding and the imbalance of power and control. Without an ongoing core-funding program from government, most voluntary organizations remain small and loosely organized, often only functioning at the "kitchen table," grassroots level. Ongoing government funding can enable an organization to develop and have a much greater impact, but it also may become dependent on that funding. At what point does funding for voluntary organizations create dependency? And is dependency necessarily a bad thing? Do limits to core funding prohibit new organizations from getting access to some of those funds and how can the funds be redistributed in a way that would be fair? These are all questions we must grapple with and I have no simple answers for them.

When we speak about capacity-building in the voluntary sector, we need to recognize that the voluntary sector is organic, with organizations rising and changing as needs arise and change, some taking root and growing and adapting and some diminishing and ultimately dying. Government's role in this process is to regulate, to provide funding for targeted services and to facilitate the overall sustainability of the sector. There are several ways governments can help voluntary organizations increase their capacity to achieve their goals. In addition to providing short-term or multi-year program funding, governments can assist with the training voluntary organizations need to operate more efficiently and professionally and reduce obstacles created by bureaucratic red tape. The Government of British Columbia is already doing both these things through the InVOLveBC program. But we can do more. It may also be possible to strengthen the third sector by seconding staff to volunteer organizations. If we seconded an employee one paid day per year to an organization, it would generate some 200,000 days or a million and a half hours of volunteer time — time that could help build civil society. If we did, would the contribution of increased human resources be as important as increased funding? How could we measure the comparative impacts? We need to work in partnership with the voluntary sector to find the answers to these questions. If we look beyond the confrontational methods some organizations use to publicize their issues, we will see that philosophical conflicts can create positive change by motivating governments to draft new legislation or policies that promote healthy, sustainable communities.

People expect governments to take responsibility for the health and safety of all citizens and they are demanding more input into developing public policy. Governments should welcome this trend because it ensures that policies and legislation have the support of their citizenry. In the same way, most volunteer organizations welcome the requirement to be accountable. Voluntary organizations enjoy a high level of public trust that they have earned throughout their conduct and record of service. The Panel on Accountability and Governance in the Voluntary Sector created in 1997 stated its objective as: "To strengthen the voluntary sector by helping the sector articulate its challenges relating to governance and accountability and developing some approaches to meeting them." One way we have done that in British Columbia is by setting up a free-standing ministry with a mandate for the volunteer sector. This means that 22,000 volunteer organizations in our province now have a voice at the Cabinet table. But this is only the beginning. There remains much more to be done and building an improved relationship between all ministries and the voluntary sector in the province.

The purpose of this conference is to bring knowledge, ideas, and philosophies together and to enlighten the dialogue on possible future directions for the partnership between public and voluntary sector. We know that this partnership is becoming increasingly important. We all acknowledge that government and the third sector must work together to achieve our common goal of improving the quality of life in our communities. This conference has focused on the voluntary and public sectors but we know that the economic side of the community and social development is also integral to this dialogue and indeed, to a civil society.

Where is the voice of the market sector in the confusion and this dilemma?[1] In the best of worlds, there can be and should be a balance between the involvement of all three sectors. The most recent figures that I have from 1997

---

[1]The 2001 second annual conference of the Public Policy and Third Sector Program at the School of Policy Studies at Queen's addressed the topic "Crossing the Divides: Voluntary, Business, Labour and Government."

indicate that voluntary organizations received 60 percent of their funding from governments, 10 percent from individuals, and 1 percent from corporations. I know that many corporations are deeply involved in the voluntary sector. I know that those figures may not include all forms of involvement and may not be an accurate representation, but it is also true though that the corporations do not by and large participate. Yet corporations have become increasingly powerful forces in our country and the world. Many transnational corporations now control more wealth than all but the largest nations in the world. With their tremendous wealth and skilled, creative employees, these corporations can make a real difference in communities.

Our challenge is to find ways to champion those in the market sector who do fund and otherwise support the voluntary sector, and to encourage the rest as corporate entities, and for them to be involved in a way that does not erode or compromise the organizations. The same caution applies to the government's role as it becomes more involved with the third sector. How can the government be more involved in the voluntary sector without really changing its nature? That is a critical question for us since people have said, time and again, "We are glad on the one hand that you have a new ministry that targets as a stand alone component in the voluntary sector, but on the other hand, we don't want you in our lives." So where is that balance and how do we create it? I believe that we need to have the three sectors of democratic society working in balance to achieve a society in which all citizens have equal opportunities for success — and then we can achieve a truly civil society.

I will leave you with a quote from Guy Tousignant. He discussed the need for collaboration and said, "It is the only way. We must make sure that we communicate with each other, we accept each other's different opinions, by listening, by looking towards the future. We all have responsibilities to make this work. Us and them does not work and attitudes must change. We can make changes that matter." I believe that. Partnership needs to be there. The shift in partnership first rests with government in our ability or inability to relinquish power and control and to believe and trust in the people who make the biggest difference in our communities, the volunteer sector, the third sector, those who care about civil society. Through the strength that comes from working with volunteers and activists with a common goal to make sure that there is progressive change in our communities, we can ensure that all people, no matter who we are, where we come from, deserving one and all (all people are deserving and we should simply say no to those who want to define people as not deserving), have a right to participate and to participate fully in all our societies.

APPENDIX A
CONFERENCE PARTICIPANTS LIST

Simon Adams. Sport and Recreation Program Advisor, Community Government and Transportation (Nunavut)

Naomi Alboim. Visiting Fellow, School of Policy Studies, Queen's University

Keith Banting. Director, School of Policy Studies, Queen's University

Dianne Bascombe. Executive Director, Centre for Voluntary Sector Research and Development

Tammy Bell. Policy Analyst, Health Canada, Ottawa

Jeannita Bernard. Director, Health Promotion and Education, Veterans Affairs Canada, Ottawa

Michel Berthiaume. Voluntary Sector Coordinator, Fisheries and Oceans Canada, Ottawa

Paddy Bowen. Executive Director, Volunteer Canada.

Kathy L. Brock. Chair, Public Policy and the Third Sector, School of Policy Studies, Queen's University

Tim Brodhead. President and CEO, The JW McConnell Family Foundation, Quebec

Lorin Busaan. Student, University of Toronto

Amy Buskirk. Program Officer, Donner Canadian Foundation, Toronto

David Cameron. Professor, Department of Political Science, University of Toronto

Angela Carr. Program Consultant, Department of Family and Community Services (New Brunswick)

Susan Carter. Executive Director, Voluntary Sector Initiative Secretariat

Bernard Chabot. Director, VOLNET Program, Industry Canada, Ottawa

Anne Charron. Group Head – Client Assistance, Charities Directorate – CCRA, Ottawa

Chantal Courchesene. Coordinator, Government Relations, Canadian Medical Association, Ottawa

Louise Delorme. Senior Advisor, Voluntary Sector Task Force, Privy Council Office, Ottawa

Glen Doucet. Senior Program Manager, Canadian Medical Association, Ottawa

Arthur Drache, QC. Partner, Drache, Burke-Robertson & Buchmayer, Ottawa

Havi Echenburg. Nonprofit, NGOs, Websites, Ottawa

Eve Elman. Associate Director, Communications, Canadian Medical Association, Ottawa

Peter Elson. Executive Director, Ontario Public Health Association, Toronto

Pat Evans. Project Officer, Canadian Institutes of Health Research, Ottawa

Susan Fletcher. Executive Director, Voluntary Sector Task Force, Privy Council Office, Ottawa

Guy Fortin. Senior Analyst, Treasury Board Secretariat, Ottawa

Mary Foster. Centre for Voluntary Sector Studies, Ryerson Polytechnic University, Toronto

Sid Frankel. Professor, Voluntary Sector Council, Winnipeg

Eva Fried. Senior Legal Policy Analyst, Industry Canada, Ottawa

Patricia Gauthier. Division de l'engagement communautaire, HRDC, Quebec

Hal Gerein. Deputy Minister, Ministry of Community Development, Cooperatives and Volunteers, BC

Roger Gibbins. President, Canada West Foundation, Calgary

Brenda Gluska. Project and Administration Manager Resource-Based Relative Value Schedule Commission, Toronto

Terry Goertzen. Special Advisor, Minister of Health, Manitoba Government

Timna Gorber. Policy Analyst, Health Canada, Ottawa

Nancy Gordon. Deputy Executive Director, CARE Canada, Ottawa

Trish Gorie. Policy Advisor, Charities Directorate, CCRA, Ottawa

Marie-France Gosselin. Coordinator, Status of Women Canada, Ottawa

Katherine Graham. Associate Dean, (Research and Faculty Development), Faculty of Public Affairs and Management, Carleton University

Georges Grujic. Senior Policy Analyst, Voluntary Sector Task Force, Ottawa

Adrian Guldemond. Professor, Ontario Alliance of Christian Schools, Ancaster

Michael Hall. Vice-President, Research, Canadian Centre for Philanthropy

Mary Elizabeth Harriman. Director, Policy Coordination External Relations, Heart and Stroke Foundation of Canada

Lori Harrop. Manager, National Children's Agency, HRDC, Hull

Al Hatton. Executive Director, National Voluntary Organisations, Ottawa

Ingrid Hauck. Director, Citizenship and Immigration Canada, Ottawa

Marilyn Hay. Regional Director General, Human Resources Development Canada, Winnipeg

Helen Hayles. Director, Volunteer Centre of Winnipeg

Tessa Hebb. President, Hebb, Knight and Associates, Ottawa

Kathryn Ann Hill. Associate Vice President, United Way of Canada/Centraide Canada, Ottawa

Liz Huff. Senior Policy Advisor, National Children's Agenda, HRDC, Hull

Barbara Humenny. Senior Analyst, Treasury Board Secretariat, Ottawa

Martin Itzkow. Director, Intersectoral Secretariat on Voluntary Sector Sustainability, Winnipeg

Llana James. Coordinator, Volunteer Resources/Community Development, Hamilton AIDS Network, Hamilton

Lois Jordan. Administrative Assistant, Defence Management Studies Program, School of Policy Studies, Queen's University

Sophie Joyal. Senior Economist, Statistics Canada, Ottawa

Gail Joyce. Assistant Executive Director, Ministry of Community Development, Cooperatives and Volunteers, Victoria

Carol Judd. Ministry of Community Development, Cooperatives and Volunteers, British Columbia

Gerda Kaegi. Professor, Ryerson Polytechnic University, Toronto

Michael Kilpatrick. Senior Policy Advisor, Ministry of Citizenship, Culture, and Recreation, Toronto

Eva Kmiecic. Deputy Commissioner, RCMP, Ottawa

William (Bill) Knight. President and CEO, Credit Union Central of Canada, Toronto

Rainer Knopff. Professor, Department of Political Science, University of Calgary

Jenny Kwan. Minister of Community Development, Cooperatives and Volunteers, BC

Diane L'Ecuyer. Director, Canada Economic Development, Hull

Blaine Langdon. Policy Advisor, Charities Directorate, CCRA, Ottawa

Nicolas Lavoie. Law Policy Analyst, Industry Canada, Ottawa

Jennifer Leddy. Legal and Policy Advisor, Canadian Conference of Catholic Bishops, Ottawa

Lona Leiren. Consultant, Carr Leiren and Associates, Edmonton

Peter Levesque. Programme Officer, CURA, Research and Dissemination Grants Programme Division-SSHRC, Ottawa

Jerry Lucas. Managing Director, Programs, Ontario March of Dimes, Toronto

Ann Mable. Partner, Marriott Mable, Wolfe Island, Ontario

Leanne Matthes. Manager, Insured Benefits, Manitoba Health, Winnipeg

Kathryn McDade. Assistant Director, National Children's Agenda, HRDC, Ottawa

Jane McGill. Director, Communications, Voluntary Sector Task Force, Ottawa

Larry McKeown. Research Associate, Canadian Centre for Philanthropy, Toronto

Joe McReynolds. CEO, Ontario Community Support Association, Toronto

Alan McWhorter. Executive Director, Kingston and District Association for Community Living, Kingston

Peter Milliken. MPP for Kingston and the Islands and Speaker of the House of Commons

Peter Mills. Policy Analyst, Voluntary Task Force, Ottawa

Jérôme Moisan. Director, patrimoine Canadien Heritage, Quebec

Patrick Monahan. Professor, Osgoode Hall Law School, Toronto

William (Bill) Murphy. Senior Tax Policy Officer, Finance Canada, Ottawa

Kathy O'Hara. Assistant Secretary, Treasury Board of Canada Secretariat, Social and Cultural Sector

John O'Leary. President, Frontier College, Toronto

Michael O'Neill. Senior Consultations Advisor, Justice Canada, Ottawa

Michael Orsini. PhD Candidate, School of Public Administration, Carleton University

Monica Patten. President and CEO, Community Foundations of Canada, Ottawa

Susan Phillips. Associate Professor, School of Public Administration, Carleton University

Helene Plante. Director, Strategic Partnerships and Alliances, Canadian Institutes of Health Research, Ottawa

Barbara Preston. Manager, Community Partnerships Program, Heritage Canada, Hull

Paul Pross. Professor Emeritus, Dalhousie University

Vivian Randell. Assistant Secretary to Cabinet (Social Policy), Executive Council of the Government of Newfoundland and Labrador

Raymond Rivet. Senior Policy Advisor, Communications, Voluntary Task Force, Ottawa

Alasdair Roberts. Professor, School of Policy Studies, Queen's University

Penelope Rowe. Executive Director, Community Services Council of Newfoundland and Labrador

John Saxby. Senior Analyst, Capacity Development, CIDA, Canadian Partnerships Branch, Hull

Phil Schalm. Program Director, Ryerson Polytechnic University, Toronto

Hugh Segal. President, Institute for Research on Public Policy, Montreal

Leslie Seidle. Director General, Privy Council Office, Ottawa

John Shields. Professor, Ryerson Polytechnic University, Toronto

Shari Silber. Analyst, Treasury Board Secretariat, Ottawa

Timothy Simboli. Executive Director, Ottawa-Carleton Family Service Centre

Roslyn Smith. Senior Advisor, Volunteer Development, Municipal and Community Affairs, NWT

Janet Snyder. Executive Director, Meals on Wheels, Ottawa

Dixon Sookraj. Okanogan University College, Kelowna

Artan Spahiu. Consultant, Foundation for International Training, Ontario

David Stevens. Barrister, Goodman and Carr LLP, Toronto

Martine Stewart. Policy Analyst, Family and Community Services, New Brunswick

John Stoker. Chief Charity Commissioner, Charity Commission of England and Wales

Wayne Stryde. Senior Analyst, Treasury Board of Canada, Ottawa

Brian Szklarczuk. Consultant, Recreation and Wellness, Culture, Heritage, and Tourism, Manitoba

Bob Thomas. President, The Thousand Islands Foundation for the Performing Arts

Patricia Thompson. Toronto

Robbin Tourangeau. Policy Advisor – Social Development, Office of the Prime Minister, Ottawa

Guy Tousignant. Secretary-General, CARE International

Karen Traversy. Senior Policy Analyst, Volunteer Sector Task Force, PCO, Ottawa

Fraser Valentine. PhD Candidate, Political Science, University of Toronto

Enikö Vermes. A/Director General, Charities Directorate, CCRA, Ottawa

Paulette Vinette. Director, Business Action Program, Toronto

John Walker. Voluntary Sector Project Office, Treasury Board Secretariat, Ottawa

Pegeen Walsh. Director, Public Policy, YMCA Canada, Toronto

Kernaghan Webb. Sessional Lecturer, Department of Law, Carleton University

David Welch. Social Planning Council of Ottawa-Carleton and University of Ottawa

Lynn Westlake. National Children's Agenda, HRDC, Hull

Deena White. Professor, Département de sociologie, Université de Montréal

Saga Williams. Health Policy Analyst, Anishinabek Health Commission, Union of Ontario Indians

Miyo Yamashita. Data Security Officer, Mount Sinai Hospital, Toronto

Todd Yates. Assistant to the Director, School of Policy Studies, Queen's University

Nadia Zurba. Program Consultant, Centre for Addiction and Mental Health, Ontario

Queen's Policy Studies
Recent Publications

The Queen's Policy Studies Series is dedicated to the exploration of major policy issues that confront governments in Canada and other western nations. McGill-Queen's University Press is the exclusive world representative and distributor of books in the series.

School of Policy Studies

Governing Food: Science, Safety and Trade, Peter W.B. Phillips and Robert Wolfe (eds.), 2001
Paper ISBN 0-88911-897-3 Cloth ISBN 0-88911-903-1

The Nonprofit Sector and Government in a New Century, Kathy L. Brock and Keith G. Banting (eds.), 2001
Paper ISBN 0-88911-901-5 Cloth ISBN 0-88911-905-8

The Dynamics of Decentralization: Canadian Federalism and British Devolution, Trevor C. Salmon and Michael Keating (eds.), 2001 ISBN 0-88911-895-7

Innovation, Institutions and Territory: Regional Innovation Systems in Canada, J. Adam Holbrook and David A. Wolfe (eds.), 2000 Paper ISBN 0-88911-891-4 Cloth ISBN 0-88911-893-0

Backbone of the Army: Non-Commissioned Officers in the Future Army, Douglas L. Bland (ed.), 2000
ISBN 0-88911-889-2

Precarious Values: Organizations, Politics and Labour Market Policy in Ontario, Thomas R. Klassen, 2000
Paper ISBN 0-88911-883-3 Cloth ISBN 0-88911-885-X

The Nonprofit Sector in Canada: Roles and Relationships, Keith G. Banting (ed.), 2000
Paper ISBN 0-88911-813-2 Cloth ISBN 0-88911-815-9

Institute of Intergovernmental Relations

Health Policy and Federalism: A Comparative Perspective on Multi-Level Governance, Keith G. Banting and Stan Corbett (eds.), 2002 Paper ISBN 0-88911-859-0 Cloth ISBN 1-55339-000-8, ISBN 0-88911-845-0 (set)

Disability and Federalism: Comparing Different Approaches to Full Participation, David Cameron and Fraser Valentine (eds.), 2001 Paper ISBN 0-88911-857-4 Cloth ISBN 0-88911-867-1, ISBN 0-88911-845-0 (set)

Federalism, Democracy and Health Policy in Canada, Duane Adams (ed.), 2001
Paper ISBN 0-88911-853-1 Cloth ISBN 0-88911-865-5, ISBN 0-88911-845-0 (set)

Federalism, Democracy and Labour Market Policy in Canada, Tom McIntosh (ed.), 2000
ISBN 0-88911-849-3, ISBN 0-88911-845-0 (set)

Canada: The State of the Federation 1999/2000, vol. 14, *Toward a New Mission Statement for Canadian Fiscal Federalism,* Harvey Lazar (ed.), 2000 Paper ISBN 0-88911-843-4 Cloth ISBN 0-88911-839-6

Canada: The State of the Federation 1998/99, vol. 13, *How Canadians Connect,* Harvey Lazar and Tom McIntosh (eds.), 1999 Paper ISBN 0-88911-781-0 Cloth ISBN 0-88911-779-9

Managing the Environmental Union: Intergovernmental Relations and Environmental Policy in Canada, Patrick C. Fafard and Kathryn Harrison (eds.), 2000 ISBN 0-88911-837-X

Stretching the Federation: The Art of the State in Canada, Robert Young (ed.), 1999 ISBN 0-88911-777-2

Comparing Federal Systems, 2d ed., Ronald L. Watts, 1999 ISBN 0-88911-835-3

John Deutsch Institute for the Study of Economic Policy

The State of Economics in Canada: Festschrift in Honour of David Slater, Patrick Grady and Andrew Sharpe (eds.), 2001 Paper ISBN 0-88911-942-2 Cloth ISBN 0-88911-940-6

The 2000 Federal Budget, Paul A.R. Hobson (ed.), Policy Forum Series no. 37, 2001
Paper ISBN 0-88911-816-7 Cloth ISBN 0-88911-814-0

Room to Manoeuvre? Globalization and Policy Convergence, Thomas J. Courchene (ed.),
Bell Canada Papers no. 6, 1999 Paper ISBN 0-88911-812-4 Cloth ISBN 0-88911-812-4

Women and Work, Richard P. Chaykowski and Lisa M. Powell (eds.), 1999
Paper ISBN 0-88911-808-6 Cloth ISBN 0-88911-806-X

Available from: McGill-Queen's University Press
Tel: 1-800-387-0141 (ON and QC excluding Northwestern ON)
1-800-387-0172 (all other provinces and Northwestern ON)
E-mail: customer.service@ccmailgw.genpub.com